'A book that clearly shows that values and auth
just nice to haves and are essential foundatioi
demonstrates the commercial benefits on the b
is fully harnessed

Sean McAuliffe,
Global Head of Business Development, The Football Association

- - - - - - - - - - - - - - -

'A strong model for leadership which takes some existing psychological
thinking on individuals and groups and moves it on further into something
unique. The result is a potent tool for clear, focused and powerful leadership.'

Professor Bruce Lloyd,
Professor of Strategic Management, Centre for International
Business Studies, London South Bank University

- - - - - - - - - - - - - - - -

'... it demonstrates that the principles behind their market leading success
in UK charity fundraising have relevance and universal application. Sector
leaders should read this book.'

Tobin Aldrich, Global Fundraising Director, Sightsavers

- - - - - - - - - - - - - - - -

'... an excellent framework for creating an organisational culture that every
manager needs to understand ... This book takes theory into practice. I
found the actionable steps laid out in an easy to follow format with clear
accompanying colour illustrations ... I discovered principles that can be applied
immediately to improve personal and organisational effectiveness.'

Mr Charles Nduka MA, MD, FRCS,
Consultant Plastic, Reconstructive and Cosmetic Surgeon

- - - - - - - - - - - - - - - -

'Refreshingly authentic and relevant to business – we could use these
principles to help us develop as individuals and unify as a group ... insights
here for everyone.'

Peter Ellingworth,
Chief Executive, Association of British Healthcare Industries

- - - - - - - - - - - - - - - -

'This is a book that can act as a bridge for many organisations to create their
own value-map, one that puts people not profit first. It encourages business to
make a deeper enquiry into what really matters – with the lightest of touch –
and encourages us all to be mindful, self-aware individuals.'

Polly Higgins,
Barrister and award-winning author of Eradicating Ecocide

To
Louise
Enjoy.
Hope you like
it. Warm
Regards,
[signature]

You can't plant
a tree in space

Dear Louise,

Thank you so much
for the support of
BHF — here's to the
partnership going from
strength to strength.

Best wishes,

Jon.

PP

PIGHOG

Designed by Livia Halmkan
Illustrated by Edward Ward

ISBN 978-1-906309-33-6
Also available as a Kindle ebook ISBN 978-1-906309-76-3

A CIP record for this publication is available from the British Library.

Pighog
PO Box 145
Brighton BN1 6YU
England, UK
info@pighog.co.uk
www.pighog.co.uk

Twitter: @Pighog | Facebook: Pighog | Pinterest: Pighog

FSC
www.fsc.org
MIX
Paper from
responsible sources
FSC® C015177

You can't plant a tree in space

Neil Hope
with
Dominic Will

Edited by Sarah Carter

Special Thanks

We would like to acknowledge the significant contributions made to this book by Nina Will and Philip Pollecoff.

Their time, intelligence, clarity and humour have played a massive role in the book's development. We are deeply grateful to them.

Particular thanks must go to Ian Langton, whose contribution, expertise and creativity were an essential component of the whole project. He has given much of his own time above and beyond the call of duty and was involved in finding effective ways to communicate the thinking a long time before this book was even conceived.

We would also like to thank our shareholders, who have shown tremendous faith and provided unwavering support through good times (and the more challenging ones!) over the last eleven years.

Our model has created one of the world's most successful fundraising companies. We lived and breathed our Unifying Principles, Philosophy and Values long before we ever put them into words, because they were embedded in our culture. They lived through and in our people.

This book is homage to those people, as we are continually amazed and inspired by the remarkable individuals that we are fortunate enough to work with every day.

CONTENTS

PREFACE

Whether you're an HR Director of a global organisation, a manager setting up a new sales force from scratch, or you're curious as to why you or your team seem to come up against the same problems again and again, the new model introduced in this book will give you the opportunity to reflect on what successful leadership looks like and how to achieve it.

The motivation for writing this book was the recognition that the majority of people feel they need to leave their humanity at the door when they come into an organisation; that somehow what we are in essence is not what is required at work. But for us, this is the starting point. If we leave what's richest about us out of our workplace, what or who do we bring in?

The Values Universe model that we introduce in this book for the first time is a way to access and embrace this richness, both for ourselves as individuals and for our organisations. It is the recognition and development of this model that has helped our organisation to grow from an idea to one of the world's leading fundraising companies employing close to 2,000 staff.

But the origins of the model took root long before HOME Fundraising was born.

Through Neil's study and practice of therapy in groups and for individuals, together with his twenty-two years' practice and teaching of meditation, he recognised again and again that people were coming up against the same kind of blocks affecting their will, drive, purpose and outcomes. Many of us get to a point in our lives where we can't move forward; there is some invisible barrier to our growth and development. We get stuck.

It was from the need to understand this invisible barrier and what it was asking of us that the Unifying Principles – a central element of the Values Universe – were developed.

The term 'Unifying Principle' is one that is used elsewhere – in science, for example. Whilst the term may be borrowed, the thinking isn't. It is unique and builds on ideas from various schools of thought, from the Greek philosophers of old to modern-day academics. In this book Unifying Principles assume that, as human beings, we all have a series of needs which have to be listened to or met. These needs – which we develop further in the context of the model and so call them Root Needs – seek to make us more present and alive. The Unifying Principles presented in our model provide a way to listen to and answer these Root Needs.

From a consideration of the needs of the individual came similar questions about groups. If as individuals we look to meet these needs and so unify and bring harmony to ourselves, how does this play out in groups? What role does the leader have in setting the conditions for the Root Needs of the group to be met? By being aware of these Unifying Principles and developing them, could the leader of the group help to avoid the invisible barriers that may cause teams to fail or fall apart?

And so we started to observe what happened within our own organisation – with the individuals, teams and leaders that are a part of it. The results are what we explore in the following pages.

Whilst we will explain the Values Universe in detail and how it works, and illustrate how you can overlay it on every aspect of your organisation, our focus is on the how and why it happens rather than providing you with endless data to prove its existence.

We give examples from our own organisation and from the wider world of psychology, sport and the arts, and demonstrate what happens when the Values Universe is ignored. We have even put in the odd graph and flow chart, but this book is not an academic study.

The works of Carl Jung, Joseph Campbell, Abraham Maslow and Roberto Assagioli were a starting point for our ideas. But the real evidence of the effectiveness of the Values Universe lies in Neil's practical experience of psychotherapy and meditation and our management of thousands of people over more than a decade within HOME Fundraising. It can be seen in our results – not just the financial ones, but also in the kind of company we have created in partnership with every individual in it. We've both been given the opportunity to develop and refine our thinking and observe what genuinely unifies, inspires and enables individuals to grow.

Towards the end of the book we encourage you to ask questions of yourselves and your teams. We know some of you will be impatient to see how our ideas can be applied. Feel free to dip into this final chapter as and when you like.

This book presents an important, innovative approach to self-development, leadership and business management. It provides a model for a new type of organisational culture – one that is purposefully cultivated and grown from within; a culture that will encourage successful leadership, develop and motivate your people over the long term and enhance profitability.

It's also a book that aims to make a positive impact on more than just the bottom line. Recognising the importance of the individual and their development within the workplace, *You can't plant a tree in space* provides the tools to create the right conditions for both you *and* your organisation to thrive.

Indeed, each of the major themes contained within this book start with an examination of the individual and their personal development before developing the concepts further to explore their impact on the organisation as a whole.

This book is therefore not a 'how to' guide that you need only apply yourself to for a minute each day. Neither is it a mere nod to the growing dialogue in business surrounding the importance of values and good corporate citizenship.

Our model goes much deeper than that.

We trace a journey through the development of the individual and their own understanding of how they influence the conditions around them, to the way groups of individuals connect and take action and apply this learning to the business environment.

Values are recognised as having an importance far beyond the superficial business currency they are often coined in, yet values alone are not the key to creating and sustaining successful organisations. For this we need to recognise and pay special attention to the system of Unifying Principles that exists in us and connects us – the individuals within any organisation – to one another. By so doing, we can build more authentic structures and thinking into the organisation itself and so drive success, sustainability and personal growth.

By setting our model down on paper, we hope that the ideas and thinking contained within it will contribute to the growing need for a new organisational culture; one that encourages authentic and considered leadership, allows individuals to bring together who they are outside the workplace with who they are inside it, and a level of interconnectedness that unites and drives people towards a common purpose. A movement that is less 'corporate' with a capital 'C' and more 'corporate' in its wider sense – related, mutual and united.

You'll note from the outset that the model has its own language and terminology. We're going to throw you in at the deep end and use it from the start but have included a glossary of key terms to help you on your way. You'll find this on the last page of the book, so that you can open it out and refer to it as you read. Stick with us, because as you read on you'll begin to see how all the individual elements we talk about come together to make our Values Universe model.

Whether you agree with all, some or none of what we set down here, the important thing for us is that our thoughts and ideas help to stimulate your own thinking around the important challenges of strong leadership and good management practice facing modern organisations. If you feel moved to contact us to share some of those thoughts, or if there is something we can help you with in your own organisation, we would love to hear from you.

Before we take you through our model, first let us introduce ourselves and take you through some of the experiences that have formed the foundation to our thinking.

INTRODUCING NEIL AND DOM

Neil Hope

I've always been deeply interested in what makes us human, believing that we should try to bring as much of ourselves as we possibly can into everything we do. I also strongly believe that essentially we are decent.

This thinking has underpinned an unusual journey. I have taught meditation practice whilst living at a Buddhist centre; got a postgraduate qualification in psychosynthesis, a form of transpersonal psychology; taught and practised as a therapist; been a sparring partner for pro boxers; been a musician; and more recently jointly run the largest fundraising company of its type in Europe, employing around 2,000 people across the UK and, at the time of writing, having raised £400 million for some of the UK's most-loved charities.

I grew up in South London in the 70s and 80s. My parents were great, home was very stable, but they were often working two jobs, so I spent most of my time with friends hanging about on the street.

On leaving the local comp with little education, despite the teaching staff's best efforts, the options were limited. The most common avenues open to us were building sites, doormen or unskilled labour. I had a range of awful jobs for a year or so; then through my friend's sister, became a salesman in a publishing firm. This seemed great at the time. I remember driving my first company car to the pub. My pals thought I'd nicked it.

I had no interest in developing my sales skills. I did, however, have an interest in and talent for showing clients a good time. By the time I was 22, I was group advertising manager. Alcohol and drugs took their toll; to say I had a dark night of the soul would be a massive understatement. I was almost entirely destroyed by them. I had no choice but to put myself back together. I started this process alone, then later took up residence in a Buddhist centre, where I lived and worked for four years, first learning, then teaching meditation practice. I was learning to create better conditions for my life internally and externally, conditions that would enable me to put myself back together, that would help me to find my place in the world. Developing mindfulness was key in this. I still have a meditation practice to this day.

After leaving the Buddhist centre I pieced together a living by playing in bands and sparring professional boxers as a warm-up for their fights. A bit of a difference to the Buddhist centre, but I found the discipline good for me and the chaps at the gym pleasant.

After a period of travelling I found my first job in fundraising; at last, something that had genuine meaning to me where I could earn money whilst helping others. Having worked at senior management level for a few years, I built a reputation for being able to grow and turn around businesses. As a result I was approached to set up what would become HOME Fundraising.

The next step was into the world of psychotherapy – having it, learning it and eventually teaching it. I found that by understanding and integrating parts of me, other deeper parts opened up and became conscious. The process of becoming a therapist and spending countless hours listening to and offering support to others helped me understand how we are deeply called to be more human. By learning to listen and respond to this, we *can* change.

I am interested in the effect that one person can have on another, what conditions are set up for good or poor relationships and how we relate to each other, not just as individuals, but also as types or even archetypes.

I'm fascinated and absorbed by exploring our humanity. I am convinced that we are more than we allow ourselves to be and not just a result of or confined by our history, though at times, for many of us, it can be hard to think otherwise. I also know that we don't have to be monks or therapists for each of us to develop our deeper, more authentic self. But uncovering it can be hard work.

A lot of years, effort and observation have gone into the creation and development of the model in this book.

I also truly believe that the discoveries we have made whilst implementing this model during the last 11 years will be of interest and use to anyone who wants a framework to help develop themselves as an individual and as an authentic, natural leader running a group, team or organisation that is infused with life, will, values and meaning.

Neil Hope

Dominic Will

I entered the world of work hungry to experience and be part of something real – a role not steeped in academia or theoretical diversion but something that had meaning and impact.

Growing up with a brother with Down's Syndrome, David, and spending many days and evenings helping my dad Michael organise doorstep collections and marshal at various fundraising events, I was very much aware of how the actions of those around you can positively impact others. I was also acutely aware that our potentials are different and believe we all deserve the opportunity to fulfil those, no matter what. On a personal level, that also meant not wasting mine.

With this in mind, it's therefore not surprising that the first door I knocked on post-university was London charity Centrepoint, an organisation dedicated to helping homeless people in the capital. The National Lottery was being launched and I knew the political landscape of the third sector was changing. To continue to grow and galvanise financial support, charities would need to become increasingly competitive and more professional. Here was a chance to experience on a voluntary basis some of those changes on the inside whilst gaining a deeper understanding of the mechanics of a large voluntary organisation and beginning to build up the necessary professional skills.

I began to form a picture of where I might fit within a third sector organisation and continued to hold this in mind when my voluntary role came to an end and I took a paid role in a City recruitment firm. A radically different environment to Centrepoint, this was a valuable experience for me, forming an important cornerstone in my commercial and financial thinking as well as presenting me with an opportunity to develop my natural ease when communicating with others. It was also during this time that I gained my black belt in judo. This was the culmination of many hard hours on the mat since childhood, and the sport remains a passion to this day, even if the knees aren't quite what they once were!

The rapid growth in the telephone fundraising market in the 90s saw the opening up of a role at National Telephone Team (NTT) that would give me the opportunity I had been looking for to build a professional career that spanned both commercial and voluntary sectors. A professional telephone fundraising agency run commercially but owned by a charity (ActionAid), NTT provided the perfect opportunity for me to bring together the things that mattered to me – positively impacting others through action, and the continued professional reform of the third sector.

That journey has continued. I have successfully united the corporate and voluntary sectors in a variety of roles – from the charity-owned commercial enterprise that was NTT, to brokering partnerships between companies and charitable causes at RNID, and devising and initiating award-winning employee engagement programmes for blue chips at the Charities Aid Foundation.

Which brings me to HOME, a natural and fitting culmination to the journey I began. HOME is a well-respected fundraising company bringing a necessary professionalism and competitiveness to the third sector whilst raising valuable charitable funds. And I'm proud to say it's not just any old fundraising company. It's now the largest professional fundraising company of its type in Europe, growing from 1% of the UK market share in 2002 to 35% today.

At times the last decade or so has been anything but plain sailing. Add to this the choppy waters that two welcome but single-minded and driven little girls have brought along the way! But I wouldn't change a thing. What we've built here at HOME through the core business and our new ventures (at home and abroad) continues to provide us all with an exciting and enriching challenge! Roll on the next decade.

Dominic Will

"Whatever YOU are,
be a **good** one."
Abraham Lincoln

VOYAGE TO
THE VALUES UNIVERSE

Our voyage together began back in 2002, when two former colleagues approached us individually to consider setting up a new venture. We wouldn't describe ourselves as typical business people – if, indeed, there is such a thing. Our backgrounds are quite diverse. We are very different people with different skill sets.

But what bound the two of us together and proved to be the glue for everything we've since done was, fundamentally, our shared sense of and interest in values.

Our voyage together has, however, taken us beyond the importance of values and prompted us to consider the factors that create harmony, motivate us and sustain success – not only in our own teams and organisation, but, we believe, within all groups and organisations.

Our experience in business, alongside Neil's long history in the study and practice of psychotherapy and meditation, has developed our appreciation that individuals and groups are formed around a series of needs – in the context of our model we call them Root Needs. When these needs are met, the groups work. We believe these Root Needs exist within all of us as humans and so within the groups and organisations we form; they demand to be acknowledged and satisfied. They are part of the human psyche – a call to us.

The Unifying Principles we have identified are a central part of our model and provide a way of satisfying these human needs. They make sense of who we are and why we are here. They represent landmarks on the journey from *the need to do* to a deepening understanding of *why we do;* they are like archetypes.

By recognising these needs exist and satisfying them through the Unifying Principles, we can develop ourselves, our teams and organisations, and so the positive influence and impact we have on those we lead and manage grows. But more on these Root Needs and Unifying Principles later.

The underlying key to positive influence and impact is our willingness and ability to be more human, more ourselves, more authentic; to humanise our organisations, and suffuse our actions and reactions with meaning and purpose.

When someone takes on the mantle of 'leader' – of a country, community, organisation, team, or even a family – we believe that a certain responsibility comes with it. A responsibility to support and genuinely care about the well-being of the group being led. A responsibility to support individuals to be themselves at their very best.

We believe that our leaders should have a positive, unifying influence in a group. It is this desire that sits at the heart of this book: for our organisations to have better leaders running better organisations, to create – if you'll permit us to make such a bold statement – a better world.

This book is about a voyage of leadership and responsibility. To some degree or another, the elements of the model are already going on in us and in our organisations right now. By being aware of and developing these elements, all leaders – in any company, group or organisation, large or small – will have a positive, unifying influence on their teams.

Alternatively, the book could be seen as a guide on how *not* to create a narcissistic, egotistical, self-congratulatory corporate dictatorship which has the potential to control and stifle all human life held within it. We guess that depends on your personal perspective of contemporary corporate culture. We, however, are never ones to sit on the fence – as this book will no doubt demonstrate.

So what's our model all about?

Values

As the carefully positioned, much-thought-about subtitle above suggests, our model starts with values.

Values are for *people*. They are what make us human. They hold our societies together; they underpin our philosophies and religions, and they are reflected in our stories, our art and our literature. Our heroes, whether Aung San Suu Kyi, Oscar Schindler or Superman, show us how to do amazing things in the world if we have the courage to live by our values. Our values come from deep within us and seek expression in thoughts and actions.

If we track back through our lives, all the significant decisions that we've taken make reference to our values – even if at times we then choose to ignore them. Because values are human, they have a part to play in every aspect of our lives, providing us with the map and compass to navigate on our voyage.

Universal and Cultural Values

In the pages that follow, we will be differentiating between what we call Universal and Cultural Values. They are an important part of the thinking that underpins our model.

Universal Values focus on core human values that just about everyone wants to live by – things like honesty, empathy, compassion, non-violence, love and tolerance. They do not depend on race, education or class.

So, when we talk about these Universal Values, we're referring to something that at a deep level all human beings seem to share. The exceptions prove the rule.

Universal Values don't isolate or exclude – they are all-embracing.

Cultural Values deeply influence what we do – what foods to eat, what clothes to buy, who to marry or shun. Cultural Values are values that we have internalised during our upbringing, often absorbing a great deal from our parents and siblings without realising it – nationality, ethnicity, religion, politics, our prejudices, stereotypes and assumptions. We celebrate our Cultural Values but we need to be careful not to let them dominate our thinking or decision-making. For, when they do, we can begin to exclude, judge and even harm others, as the traditions of some cultures, and their beliefs and practices, are less recognised and respected than others.

We believe it is important to *celebrate* our Cultural Values but act and *re-act* according to our Universal Values – both in our personal and professional lives.

Values in organisations

We're interested in how values affect us as individuals, our societies and the organisations we work within; how they can form the foundations for leaders and managers to bind teams and groups together.

People with shared values share *intent*. Universal Values can connect us very directly to the deep and often unconscious *shared intent* or *Will* of the group. The connection between Universal Values and the Will to act is the part of us that created our society, from cities to civilisations, from law to economics and science to religion. It is the active expression of our values that has created the structures that we know as human.

Over centuries, the engine of Will based on our Universal Values has transformed society – from the development of liberal democracy to the abolition of slavery, from the Civil Rights Movement to improved child protection. And this force can be harnessed in just the same way to transform our organisations.

The challenge of capitalism is to ensure that free markets behave with a moral compass – a challenge that has been with us at least since the flotation of the East India Company in 1698!

Over the last 11 years, we have set up and managed hundreds of teams of different sizes and levels of responsibility, and grown from five members of staff to around 2,000. When our company has struggled in one way or another, we have been able to unify our teams and return to profitability by being more conscious of Universal Values and the five Unifying Principles outlined in this book.

However, in many organisations the values we hold as individuals are put aside and are considered the preserve of leisure time. Work is work – the tough business of survival – and our values, like our appreciation of art or wine or literature, are to be left at the door to be collected on our way out.

So if **values** are us, the things that define us and
make us **uniquely human,**
what does it say that in many of our
workplaces, where we spend the
greatest portion of our lives, **our
humanity is set aside** because it
might just get in the way?

In the last few years we've been bombarded with stories of organisations and businesses carrying on in a way that dehumanises us. Many of us no longer buy the idea that all a business has to do is make money.

This dismissal of values in business can be catastrophic. Consider the near collapse of the worldwide banking system in recent times. As we know, very few leaders paid attention to the tell-tale signs that global recession was looming, and those that did were largely ignored.

It would, of course, be unfair to suggest that all business is devoid of values. A quick internet search will reveal page after page of websites sporting ethical credentials and philosophies that position quality and best practice at the heart of their companies.

However, we're not talking about values enshrined in corporate statements. These types of values quite often have very little to do with the actual day-to-day working environment. An organisation that might aspire through its values to 'treat others with respect' may unwittingly create a culture that is far from respectful. We've all worked in places where 'what it says on the tin' – in an interview or in the company brochure – doesn't apply in reality.

But before anyone gets confused by all this 'values' talk and mistakenly assumes us to be on some sort of Corporate Social Responsibility (CSR) mission, let us state now that this book is absolutely *not* a meditation on CSR.

Of course, we believe businesses should be good corporate citizens and have a positive influence over their communities and supply chains. But all too often organisations attempt to do this by applying external solutions – PR, training or communications – rather than looking for the deeper, longer-term answers that lie internally.

A model for a new organisational culture

An organisation built on Universal Values is likely to prosper, attract and retain great people. But we recognised early on that values alone are not the answer.

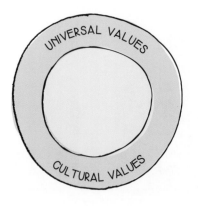

The model starts with Universal and Cultural Values. It recognises the inclusive, all-embracing nature of Universal Values.

For Universal Values to become more than a nice idea or just associated with organisations with a charitable or social remit, something else needs to be in play. Without the robust and workable framework of an organising set of Principles and a Philosophy, Universal Values in isolation will struggle to have a positive influence on the practical output and actions of an individual or organisation.

Indeed, without leaders being mindful and reflective using a template against which they can measure their own decisions, behaviour and actions, many of our organisations can become – are becoming – distorted. In a very real sense, they are becoming sick.

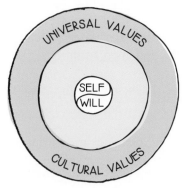

Just having values doesn't necessarily connect us to our Self and Will or to the Will of the group. We need something to build a bridge between our values and how we express and act upon them through our Self and Will.

The model outlined in this book offers such a template, one that encourages leaders to ask important questions of themselves and their teams.

Indeed, as we began to discover and develop the Values Universe for ourselves, there were many questions it encouraged us to ask of our own business and the individuals in it. For example:

● Why can some people run bigger groups than others?

● Why do great team leaders disintegrate when asked to manage larger groups?

● What determines an individual's level of 'buy-in' to the organisation?

- Why does one leader seem to unify a group and another distort or destroy it?

- Why do some teams seem be full of drive and others Will-less and lazy?

- Is there a direct correlation between 'buy-in' and performance?

- Does 'buy-in' have a greater degree of influence over performance than responsibility or salary?

The Values Universe model brings together our hands-on experience of psychology, philosophy and running a business and is a way of highlighting and being more conscious of what is already going on within the psyche of individuals and in organisations.

The elements that make up the Values Universe work just as well for individuals as they do for leaders and entire organisations.

We began to notice that the deeper problems in the business were most frequently caused when the manager was unable to offer a strong centre to the team. Something about their depth, maturity and drive - or lack or it - was directly affecting team-dynamics and therefore the manager's ability to lead effectively. The team would then seem to distort and the subpersonalities in the individuals would take over and undermine the group. These are parts of us that have been formed since birth in order to respond to various difficulties or demands. Examples include the critic, people pleaser, judge, hero, listener, carer, victim or saboteur.

Subpersonalities organise themselves around a need within the psyche.

More and more we realised that the importance of the manager and the dynamic with their staff was crucial to the success of the company. We started to look for a maturity and depth in management, which could be reflected back to our staff, as without this the results proved unsustainable.

We began to notice that the deeper problems of the business were most frequently caused by the manager either relying too heavily on interpersonal relationships or being all-consumed by process, disassociating from their staff completely and spending too much time *managing* rather than *doing* – after all, there are a huge number of tasks to be completed when you have responsibility for a large number of individuals.

If the business was to grow successfully, we needed to find a way of dealing with these fundamental issues. Commercial USPs and some Herculean efforts would not be enough. In order to scale up, we needed a consistency and clarity of approach.

The Values Universe model gave us both.

As you read on, we'll show you how the model is divided into different layers that already exist within every individual and that, by focusing our attention and meeting the needs of each of these layers in turn, we can unlock our potential.

Meeting the Root Needs of the individual and the group

In his 1954 book *Motivation and Personality,* Abraham Maslow came up with a model of individual human needs, often shown as a pyramid – with our most basic needs at the bottom and self-actualisation at the top.

Maslow believed that once our most basic and fundamental needs are met – food, water, shelter, etc. – we become aware of new, higher needs that, once also met, reveal yet further more refined needs.

The concept is used frequently by creative and marketing agencies to emphasise that clients need to position their products in such a way as to meet the higher needs and aspirations of their customers as well as the lower ones. If you use advertising to suggest that the new sausage roll you're marketing will instigate deeply loving, secure personal relationships, you're likely to get wider buy-in than if you simply appeal to their greed and love of junk food. It's all about how much influence you feel you can attribute to a product in terms of the needs it can meet for the buyer.

Our experience has taught us that, regardless of how Maslow's ideas have been put to use in the marketing world, his model of needs is very real.

But there is also another set of needs that *can't* be met by the external world – what our model calls Root Needs.

These other needs are experienced internally as deep yearnings or callings. We don't mean hankerings you might have for a holiday home in the South of France, or a little sports car on the drive. Listen to these by all means, but it's not the same thing. Here, we're talking about deeper parts of ourselves that have to be integrated into the whole of us in order for the psyche to mature. These Root Needs include:

- the **practical** need to *do*

✦ the need for identity – our **personality**

✦ the need to understand our place in the world, our **purpose** and where we're going

✦ the **psychological** need to be whole

✦ and the need for deeper **philosophical** meaning.

Ultimately, these needs seek to provide a way for our core selves to live fully in the world, to meet our full potential. They seek to make us fully alive, fully ourselves, fully aware and fully engaged in our existence and the world around us.

This is not the need to be 'perfect', far from it. But it is the need to be perfectly us.

In the same way we as individuals have the need to develop and to be whole, so too we look to the groups we are part of and the leaders of those groups to help us meet these Root Needs.

We all have an idea of how we want our leaders to behave — even if these expectations are unconscious — and the larger the group, the larger the need for a solid leader. If that need is not met, then the consequences can be far-reaching. Think about Winston Churchill and his strength of leadership during the Second World War, or JFK's courageous leadership in the 60s to bring about the Non-Proliferation Treaty with the USSR.

If we as leaders are to meet our own Root Needs and all the needs of our groups and the individuals in them, we need to know ourselves and be able to trust ourselves at a deep level. To meet the needs of the group we are leading, we have to be present, bring our authentic selves to the task and know what to look for.

Unifying Principles

The five Unifying Principles which we believe are already present deep within the human psyche, develop in us when meeting these Root Needs. They are the:

- **Practical Principle**
- **Personality Principle**
- **Purpose Principle**
- **Psychological Principle**
- **Philosophical Principle**

These five Unifying Principles reflect a 'natural' leadership and management style and answer the Root Needs that we all have on the voyage, from the practical need to *do* to the ultimate need for deeper philosophical meaning.

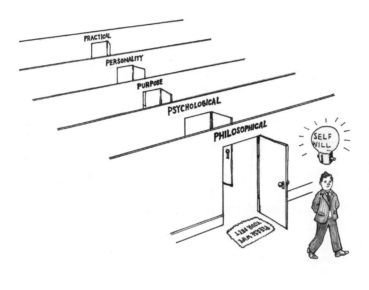

Our observation of the Unifying Principles goes back a long way. We have realised their potential by noticing and developing the tens of thousands of individuals we have employed, the teams we have watched succeed and those that have not done so well.

At times they are hidden and unconscious but, nevertheless, they already exist. They are not just relevant to business; **they apply all the time to everything.** The Values Universe model only serves to highlight their existence, make us more aware and conscious of them and so more likely to utilise them in our day-to-day lives.

As we understand, live and work by one **Unifying Principle,** another opens up. Each one offers a **gateway to the next.**

The five Unifying Principles enable us to make the connection between our values and our own Self and Will.

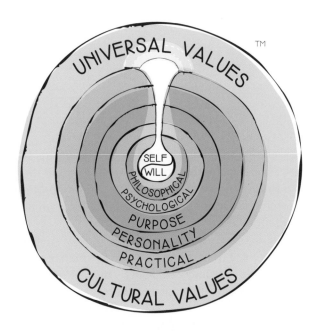

Whereas an individual working at the first two levels of the Principles – Practical and Personality – can work brilliantly within a small group, someone managing larger groups will need to integrate Purpose, Psychological and, ultimately, the Philosophical Principle to optimise their own success and that of the group.

They are **not** Principles that people **choose to adopt** or not; they are like **archetypes** and are already alive **within all of us** to some degree or another – if not at **work,** then at **home;** if not as **managers,** then perhaps as **parents.**

Trust the Unifying Principles
They are already part of us

In our experience, these Unifying Principles govern an individual's ability to lead and influence any group with clarity and insight. By being more conscious of and integrating each of them, our natural influence grows, as we create greater harmony and direction in the groups we lead, ensuring they remain fulfilled, engaged and motivated.

That's not to say that each and every manager within the organisation needs to work at all levels – but certainly those at the top need to be aware of and aspire to them.

Even an awareness of the Principles will benefit you, both in yourself – the way you feel, act, think – and in the way you are perceived by others in the groups and organisations you are part of as others begin to sense in you qualities they can trust, rely on and follow.

For us at HOME, there was a direct correlation between working with the Unifying Principles and being able to expand. Without building the Unifying Principles into the very core of the business, we would have spent an exhausting amount of time trying to establish a foothold and set Conditions in ever-changing situations.

All this was going on between 2006 and 2009. We were working 18-hour days, moving from 200 to 1,000 staff and setting up 50 different teams, so we really needed to ensure we were growing in the way we wanted to grow. We needed to develop a common language and common reference points between Southampton and Bristol, Newcastle and Edinburgh.

You may have experienced this, or perhaps you are living through these challenges right now?

Very early on, we realised that we had to work at a human level rather than a corporate level. Today we have around 2,000 staff and more than 300 teams. The Unifying Principles enabled us to get it right – not always first time, we're not going to pretend we're perfect. But even when things weren't quite as they should have been, when teams showed signs of breaking down, Unifying Principles meant that we knew where we had to look to put things right.

One thing that always strikes people coming into our organisation for the first time is how young our senior managers are. People attending our annual conference are often surprised that many of our managers are young people in their 20s who haven't been to university, have little formal education and yet are responsible for managing teams of over 100 people. And they do this with great skill and maturity, enjoying high levels of respect from their team members. These managers stay with our organisation for years and, as a result, we don't experience the huge staff turnover that other organisations in our industry might experience. This wasn't always the case. We believe our Values Universe model, and the Unifying Principles at the heart of it, are playing a key part in that achievement.

Working to the model, internalising and modelling the five Unifying Principles gives all our staff a language through which they can understand and experience the process and stages of maturing required for all responsible leadership. As such we have little time for the all-too-frequent pernicious arguments that dismiss the capabilities and potential of young people in contemporary society. We have taken great pleasure in watching the development and impact of individuals who many politicians or commentators would likely have written off. We are also very proud of the positive ripple-effects that the many thousands of people we have employed over the years will have/have had on the wider economy as they take the skills learned at HOME on to other jobs and industries.

Unifying Principles enable us to diagnose where we are going wrong, as well as problems in groups and organisations. We can clearly see what's missing, what they lack and what they have in abundance. They are like five notes played as a chord – we become so familiar with the sound of the chord and with each individual note that contributes to the complete sound that, when we visit our teams or regions or when we work with departments, we can immediately hear which note it is that's missing.

Each Unifying Principle looks to bring parts of us as individuals, teams and organisations together. If they are not recognised and worked on within the group, then both the groups and the individuals in them have the potential to distort. Organisations are particularly at risk because the turmoil caused by a lack of self-awareness and by ignoring the Unifying Principles is so much more obvious in a group – especially a group where the focus can primarily and mistakenly be placed solely on financial profit. As Roger Steare (2009) points out:

'If personal morality is challenging, professional and business ethics is infinitely more demanding because of the complexities of having so many other people's interests represented in the workplace.'

The findings of neuroscience and psychology show that much of what happens when people get together is unconscious. In groups, the unconscious is highlighted in a way that we would never spot if we were on our own.

These five Unifying Principles help ensure the leaders and managers we work with and the groups they influence are able to communicate successfully and embody Universal Values and a Philosophy authentically through their actions. They offer a Unifying Centre around which leaders can bring groups together, and a way to be mindful, to reflect, to model to others and trigger the Will of individuals and the organisation as a whole as they connect to our fundamental Root Needs.

The term 'Unifying Centre' is most often used in psychotherapy where the therapist is seen as an external Unifying Centre for their client:

> 'Initially there is pain, discomfort or crisis for most individuals seeking counselling. They have no internal reference point, no stable sense of identity and often feel victims to the forces of their own psyche. Like a leaf tossed by the wind, they feel no capacity for clear awareness and vision, for being the *source and sustenance* of their existence. They have no stable centre of identity ... The psychosynthesis counsellor will be willing to provide an *external unifying centre* for the client, until the client is able to establish *an internal unifying centre* for herself.'
> (Whitmore, 2000)

In our company, we have adapted the term for use within the workplace – not that we expect our managers to be therapists or, indeed their team members to be in crisis; far from it. However, we do ask our managers to be a Unifying Centre for the members of the team; a safe, objective, reliable centre which models the appropriate Unifying Principle to their team so that those individuals can then recognise, habitualise and internalise the Principle for themselves.

Unifying Centre
The Unifying Centre is the stable centre of the group. An individual will be the Unifying Centre of a group when they have recognised, habitualised and internalised the Unifying Principle in themselves. At this point they can model the Unifying Principle needed back to the rest of the group.

Together, Universal Values and a Philosophy that expresses them (something we look at in Chapter 3), accompanied by Unifying Principles, will enable less superficial, more centred decisions to be made. The combination provided by the Values Universe model will allow us to deepen our thinking, our intentions, include more of ourselves in what we do and even, dare we say it, pave the way for wisdom.

We can then include more of ourselves in the workplace.

Work becomes not just a place for practical action mixed with unconscious emotion, but a place where we can speak and act according to our Universal Values and Philosophy. We are guided by Unifying Principles.

And, of course, this influence isn't just about those at the very top of an organisation. It will also be reflected in the general psychological well-being of those in any position of responsibility.

The Values Universe exists deep within every group, organisation and individual. The model works personally, professionally and financially, delivering sustainable results. But it needs to be modelled continually; not doing so is the biggest risk to any business.

In the next chapter, **Conditions,** we look at how every organisation and every individual develops within a context. Just as you can't plant a tree in space, you can't create an organisation's culture in a vacuum. We consider the Conditions an organisation needs in order to be successful and how central the mindful, authentic and self-aware leader is to that success. We examine how a leader takes responsibility for their own mental states and how they engage and inspire their teams.

In *Chapter Three,* **Values and Philosophy,** we explore Cultural and Universal Values and how central they are to humanity, to us as individuals and in the context of groups. We then explore the importance of grounding a whole organisation in a value system. We look at the way those values can be expressed through an organisational Philosophy and through the thoughts and deeds of everyone within it.

We illustrate how destructive **distortions** can be when we prioritise Cultural Values over Universal Values and how these distortions can lead many companies and industries to fail. In the context of this book, we define distortions as a deviation from Universal Values, Unifying Principles and our authentic Self. Their effect (intended or unintended) is to block, stifle and divert us from our human potential.

In *Chapter Four,* **Unifying Principles, Leadership and Influence,** we explore the five Unifying Principles that are central to our model. By internalising these specific leadership Principles, harmony, drive and a common goal can be brought about within organisations. The result will be mindful, natural leaders who can set the right Conditions for organisations, making them stronger, better places to work, with more positive outcomes.

And as you read on you'll discover these five Unifying Principles are multi-dimensional, operating across the interrelated yet distinct areas of:

➤ individual development

➤ natural/authentic leadership

ε organisational change

Across each of these chapters we will also explore the concept of the authentic Self and the idea of Will; how we develop a strong sense of Self by being mindful and how that connects with individual and collective Will. And just like a person, the more authentic an organisation is, the greater sense of Self it has; the stronger it is. Note that the Values Universe depicts the Self and Will at the centre of the model, illustrating that an organisation working to Universal Values through the framework of the Unifying Principles will enable the Will of the individual and the group to be positively triggered.

Finally in *Chapter Five,* **Embarking on Your Own Voyage,** we look at the various ways in which the Values Universe can be applied and how we can recognise, habitualise and internalise the model and the five Unifying Principles. We summarise how you can put our model into practice in your own organisation over the long term.

By establishing the Values Universe at the heart of your organisation – a system that is both visible and visceral, felt and embodied throughout every level of the business – you awaken the huge potential of each individual and the organisation.

We hope you'll gain an insight into how our model has been shaped and refined over the years as well as stimulating your own thinking. Above all else, we're confident we can provide you with a practical, relevant model that can steer your organisation towards sustainable success.

Marigolds and meditation

Part of life as a Western monk was teaching meditation to members of the public looking to slow their minds down a bit and get a bit more in touch with themselves and their patterns. Occasionally we were asked to hand out our brand of wisdom to a determined seeker of enlightenment but, thank goodness this was rare, as there truly wasn't a vast amount to go around.

This all took place in the South London Buddhist Centre, where I lived. There were fourteen of us in the Centre, all men, sharing rooms in a large four-storey Victorian property in the heart of Clapham.

That's Clapham, London. Not the Himalayas or Dharamsala, the Ganges or Thailand. Clapham. Even though I had completely changed my life, I had only managed to move a few miles from where I grew up.

In an environment where there was no television, alcohol, loud music or constant stimulation, it was tough. I soon got to know myself and what kind of state I was in. We rose early to pray or practise together, spent much of our time in silence, had little or no money, few clothes, and relationships outside were sometimes hard to sustain.

I was lucky my family were great, unlike my friends who pretty much thought I'd completely lost the plot. They thought that before long they would see me dancing down Streatham high street in London surrounded by drums and bells, wearing a loincloth.

I tried to explain that this seemed like a good place to get myself together; that millions of people throughout Asia were committed Buddhists and that they seemed to have absolutely no interest in converting anyone to anything. To be honest, I wasn't even sure if I was a Buddhist!

I explained that the bookshelves where I was living were full of books from other beliefs and each one was read, studied and treated with great respect. I liked this, I explained ... and as yet I hadn't been asked to give over money or be part of some weird membership ritual involving spontaneous and embarrassing singing.

The more I talked, the more my old pals seemed to want to punch me in the face. Clearly bemused and wondering who they had to threaten in order to drag me from this terrible place, they seemed not to appreciate that it was just me: same bloke, same background.

It was not an easy place to live. Despite the external face we presented, harmony didn't always reign. Just practising to not kill at least two of my fellow peace-loving brethren was enough to convince me that I would one day eventually reach enlightenment. Frankly, it couldn't be any harder than this.

Meetings between us all would last hours. Vital issues like broccoli, carrots or the washing-up would often incite an argument. Of course, this was all framed in the context of being completely 'spiritual'.

'I would appreciate it if the community would practise mindfulness with more diligence,' was one of our favourite phrases.

'Frankly, I'd appreciate it if you would piss off or buy a dishwasher ...' I thought, as I nodded along, trying not to look disgusted at our lack of spiritual effort.

There was nothing more annoying than hearing someone bang on about the inferior quality of the washing-up, and how the community needed to get a grip, before they then stormed off upstairs to the Buddhist Centre, where a class sat silently waiting for their meditation teacher to arrive, at which point that same person instantly turned into Gandhi.

Especially when that person was me ...

I practised a lot of meditation, several hours a day. I needed to. Various mindfulness, compassion and insight practices were all designed to quieten the mind at deeper and deeper levels.

In the same way exercise leads to fitness or yoga encourages flexibility, so meditation leads to mindfulness. Of course, these are only foundations. If we never moved outside of our 30 minute run or yoga practice, we wouldn't stay in shape. The same applies with meditation. Practising mindfulness outside of the context of meditation is vital. The relationship between the practice and the conditions we set in the rest of our lives is vital. The more we practise mindfulness, the more we become aware of the conditions we are creating from moment to moment out of our habits and intentions. If we meditate, then fill our minds full of crap then the effects of our meditation will be limited.

I was lucky to meet a handful of people during this time who seemed as though they had really got somewhere with themselves. I became very interested in what they all had in common.

This, I found, had nothing to do with Buddhism or even meditation, but was based on human principles that I later found in people from many other beliefs and disciplines, including psychotherapy.

The individuals all seemed to manifest these principles in the way they lived. They also seemed to have worked on the art of listening to and trusting their psyche and what it presents to them, rather than dragging it around by the neck like a reluctant dog on a lead.

They seemed to exude a harmony, confidence and a kind of gravitas which brought a feeling of focus and reassurance to every situation they were in. Also, they didn't sit around waiting for divine inspiration. They seemed fully engaged in their work, relationships, practice and all other aspects of their lives. It became clear after spending a lot of time with these few individuals that they were more in touch with and able to respond to a fundamental human need in themselves: the need to be fully authentic, fully alive and with a belief that they and others have unlimited potential. Along with this, little time seemed to be wasted on bolstering their ego or protecting themselves from difficult thoughts or feelings.

Most of all they seemed to be able to bring a real depth of focus and meaning to even the most mundane of tasks. Meanwhile the rest of us mortals seemed to get tripped up by unconscious forces asserting themselves, forces which would cause us to suddenly behave strangely over broccoli, carrots, washing-up and the like. At different points each of us would hit a wall – the same wall where something just stopped working. This would often cause individuals to give up on themselves and the idea that they could be more.

It was during this period of time that through observation I began asking certain questions:

- Is there part of the psyche that will naturally seek to find harmony or unify aspects of itself given the right conditions?

- If the psyche does naturally look to unify itself, does it do so gradually, as a whole or in levels?
- Do we as humans build up levels or layers in the psyche like a safe and secure platform that we return to when needed?
- Is there a natural calling or need to find these levels?
- How do these look in groups?

Indeed, over 20 years later these questions continue to grip me and have created the foundations for the Unifying Principles in this book.

Despite the image of enlightened beings sitting on sharp rocks in the snow sporting a mere loincloth and going without food or moving for months on end, meditation and mindfulness are on one level very practical tools.

I personally never actually gave up food, and I wore clothes, keeping my loincloth for best. Indeed, if only my food intake had been more limited: boiled something on a bed of something that tasted of nothing wasn't anything to get excited about.

As I sat quietly in my loincloth in Clapham on a sharp rock in the garden, having eaten nothing but dirt and air for months, I felt a deep intuition coming to consciousness ...

Suddenly I had the answer ...

... then I forgot it.

"Success is a science;
if you
have the **conditions,**
you get the
result."

Oscar Wilde

CONDITIONS

Individuals

If we take the time to look back over our lives and reflect upon some of the decisions we've made along the way, there is no doubt we will begin to trace pathways between these and where we find ourselves, the type of people we are, how we think and feel about ourselves and the world around us, the types of relationships we have and even the jobs we do.

Maybe we had loving parents as we grew up and, from this, feel we have a good understanding of what constitutes a deep and meaningful relationship. Maybe we went to a good school, where we learned in safety and were encouraged to progress, or maybe the opposite was true.

Whatever our background, our experiences will have also been influenced by other more deep-rooted internal factors, such as our genetic and biological make-up, our natural drives to know and relate to others and our value systems. Our genetic predisposition will have determined to some extent how we experienced school, and how we experienced school will have shaped us as adults.

Of course, our choices are more limited when we are younger. As we get older we have a greater capacity to choose how we let those early experiences influence the course of our lives. We become more aware of the Conditions we are setting for ourselves for the future and that we have a certain amount of power to affect situations all the time. These choices are fundamentally affected by our mental states, which in turn fundamentally affect our choices – a potentially negative cycle if those mental states and choices are negative.

Conditions include the external, internal, mental, emotional, genetic, social and historical influences which contribute to the situation and circumstances we currently find ourselves in.

So, given the importance of both external and internal Conditions and the fact that each are interrelated, where do we start?

The best place to begin is with ourselves. Our awareness and the way we think are an essential part of setting Conditions for ourselves and those around us.

"Life is a sum of all your choices."

Albert Camus

Most of us lead full and busy lives. We can be constantly distracted in a bid not to feel uneasy, anxious or depressed and allow ourselves to unwittingly worsen the Conditions in our lives. In our perpetual 'doing' cycles, we continue to make the same mistakes over and over again without taking time to understand what we are doing and why. Without the right combination of action and reflection, we risk not recognising or understanding the Conditions we are setting ourselves.

And we are constantly setting and re-setting Conditions – both consciously and unconsciously, aware or unaware – to get the results we want in our thoughts, in our actions, in what we do, in what we don't do, in how we are and who we are.

But one thing's for certain: there's no such thing as *not* setting Conditions.

Nothing happens in a **vacuum** –
no conversation, interaction or transaction.
You can't plant a tree in space.

Discovering your own Conditions

Imagine that you've written your life story and it's about to hit the shops. A journalist from the *Times Literary Supplement* is on the phone and wants you to give a quick summary of the book. He's only got a few minutes so you'll have to work quickly and intuitively. (Remember there are no right or wrong answers to his questions, so accept the first answers that come to mind and go with those.) You'll find it most useful to write these down before feeding them back to him. He asks:

- What is the title of your story?
- What kind of story is it: happy, sad, heroic, tragic, interesting, boring? Use your own words.
- Now, in a few sentences describe the closing scene – how does your story end?

According to Eric Berne, the founder of Transactional Analysis (TA), a model for understanding human personality, relationships and communication, we have all pretty much written our life stories by the time we are 12 years old. Maybe not on paper and maybe without realising it, but we've all penned a story for ourselves that we unconsciously hold in mind throughout our lifetime. This story sets the Conditions for the decisions we make in life and the actions we take as, without awareness, we live out the story we have written for ourselves to its final conclusion. Reflection and mindfulness give us the chance to become aware of, and rewrite where necessary, that story.

(This exercise is adapted from Stewart & Joines, 2012)

57

> "People come to work as human beings and unless you get that you'll never be a leader."
>
> Heather Rabbatts, CBE

Leaders

In organisations the moral fibre of our leaders is constantly in question – leaders who are more than willing to cash in on a huge annual bonus but not so willing to accept responsibility for poor performance and unethical practice.

Senior people within our organisations need to be applying a good degree of wisdom, maturity and self-knowledge in their decision-making. Frankly, if they have none, then the greater the distortions will be.

The Values Universe model expects leaders to know themselves and their subpersonalities and neuroses, to be mindful, because we all know that acting out of lack of awareness can be catastrophic for the rest of us. The Unifying Principles are all about developing that awareness. By becoming more personally aware, we can change how we see, lead, inspire and engage teams and organisations, and how those teams see and respond to us.

For when a team or group of people feel they cannot express or be themselves, there is a risk that group will ultimately disintegrate or turn against the leader and distortions will occur.

To achieve better lives, with deeper, richer relationships, better leaders and better organisations, we need to invest more of our time, effort and attention into thinking, speaking and acting in ways that are conducive to creating the right Conditions.

If we as individuals, our children, communities and organisations, are not thriving it is because the Conditions set for each of them – past and present – are not enabling that to happen. We are not rooted in the right soil; we have become the tree in space, starved of all the Conditions that enable us to reach fruition.

"This being, that becomes;
On the arising of this, that arises.
This not being, that does not become;
On the cessation of this, that ceases"

The Pāli Canon

This fundamental law set out in one of the earliest Buddhist scriptures, the Pāli Canon, holds the universe together.

And, of course, so it does within our organisations.

Leaders, teams and organisations set good and bad Conditions for themselves by the degrees of awareness applied to tasks, relationships, decisions, even the thinking in meetings. This awareness – or lack of it – then impacts the habits and outcomes of our organisations.

At HOME, for example, we are always keen to ensure that fundraisers and team leaders do not focus purely on the outcomes of their role, for example the number of sign-ups they are targeted to achieve by the end of the day or week. By focusing purely on the outcomes, they start to let their good habits slip. They start to focus on extraneous factors, like it being 'the wrong time of day' to sign someone up, or that houses with red doors and gnomes in the gardens are hopeless and shouldn't be approached, rather than staying focused on having quality, human conversations with every person they come into contact with now, in the present. They start to lose sight of the training they have received, the skills they have developed, and focus instead on where they need to be by the end of the day or week rather than the here-and-now.

It's similar to running a marathon. Someone wouldn't run every moment of it thinking, 'I have to run 26 miles'. They'd never make it. It would feel too daunting. They focus instead on how they're feeling now, what they need to do in the moment to adjust their pace, to lessen the pain, to quench their thirst. If the focus was constantly on the finish line, they'd probably not make it that far.

It's the same in business. We don't – or at least shouldn't – start a business by saying we want to earn a million pounds and work backwards from there. We set the foundations and Conditions first. Success and sustainability are more likely that way.

At HOME we have developed a management tool called HOME's House that enables us to assess every aspect of the Conditions within our organisation. HOME's House is made up of different areas including foundations, activity, follow-up, praise and recognition. Each area has a percentage attached to it, indicating the amount of time that needs to be spent on each so our managers and staff don't get too caught up in either one thing or another.

HOME'S HOUSE

Many managers and teams spend the highest percentage of their time on Activity – but this is not where the results are.

For example, in the past we have found that many of our managers and their deputies have spent too much time caught up in activity. Little attention is given to follow-up (where we have found the results to be), or too much time given to praise and recognition.

Within our own organisation, HOME's House has become an easily recognisable system, a tool for analysis of the current Conditions being set by individuals, teams, regions or the organisation as a whole. It encourages managers to be aware of how much emphasis they should put on what. It shows them where to look for problems and where they might be lacking. Whether it's Human Resources, Client Services or the Operations side of the business, our senior managers will always be aware of the Conditions they and others are setting.

We have a saying at HOME: 'If in doubt, think HOME's House.' Okay, maybe it's not the greatest of sayings. It's probably not up there with 'A stitch in time saves nine' or 'A bird in the hand is worth two in the bush'. We believe that all organisations would benefit from a similar measurement and analytical tool that they can easily refer to when it becomes clear that Conditions need re-setting.

Who we want to be and what we want our organisations to be depends on how we recognise, understand and choose to alter and set Conditions. We can do this both internally, in our ability to reflect and by developing our self-awareness, and externally, through our actions. Safe to say that the Conditions we're setting for ourselves won't be that great if we spend all our time drinking vodka in a bathtub watching *The Texas Chainsaw Massacre* on a loop.

Central to our ability to set Conditions are the concepts of interdependence, Self, Will and mindfulness.

Let's begin with those.

*Inter*dependence

Interdependence is the understanding that nothing happens in isolation; that there is a complex series of connections between everyone and everything. From our mental states to our actions, their outcomes and the intricacies of the relationships we have with one another, even the places we live and the air we breathe.

Nowhere is this clearer than within an ecosystem where we recognise that all living things depend on one another for their continued survival. Some of the relationships are direct, some of them are indirect. And this is so for all of us on every level of our being, including our current and previous mental states and relationships. And it's complex, because the roots of all the Conditions we are dealing with are not necessarily of our own making.

But how we respond to these Conditions is.

In our organisation, this concept allows us to appreciate that we can't always change people's behaviour or situations in seconds. We need to be aware of all the interconnected areas before Conditions can be re-set. We can't look at things in isolation and think that if we fix that one thing everything will suddenly fall into place. We look at our whole organisation, as many other organisations already do, in the light of interdependence.

There are many subtle examples of how this will work within business, but an obvious example within HOME is that the number of sign-ups our business gets – as in all organisations to a greater or lesser extent – is not just down to the people talking directly to potential donors. We don't send our fundraisers out in isolation and expect financial returns – they are vital to us, we are vital to them. The relationship between the two is essential and will determine the outcomes. Our individual fundraisers need to feel connected and that they are part of something.

So when someone is out trying to sign up donors at 8.30pm on a cold winter's night, they are not alone; they are in constant communication with others within the organisation. We send them messages to motivate them, we update them, make them laugh, give them competitions to take part in. There are magazines in which people share their experiences, company films to inspire, engage and congratulate, regular updates on results and where we are. There are ongoing dialogues and bets between regions – all done in good humour and to help set the right Conditions.

Every individual fundraiser feels part of something bigger. They become more interested and engaged in what is going on around them, in who's doing what and how. They become genuinely interested in the business and its success and not just their own individual input. They are encouraged to think interdependently as we model it all around them.

To really lay the Conditions for better experiences and outcomes, we need to understand and appreciate the complex and interdependent nature, not only of business, but of life. As Martin Luther King said in his 1967 'Christmas Sermon on Peace':

'We are all caught in an inescapable network of mutuality, tied together into a single garment of destiny. Whatever affects one directly, affects all indirectly. We are made to live together because of the interrelated structure of reality. Before you finish eating breakfast in the morning, you've depended on more than half the world. This is the way our universe is structured, this is its interrelated quality.'

Quite simply, everything exists in relation to something else. Even us.

"It Really boils down to this: **that all Life is interrelated."**

Dr Martin Luther King, Jr

Developing the Self

'Be true to yourself' is a mantra which has an almost mindless simplicity to it. Everyone from Shakespeare's Polonius to the Spice Girls, our teachers or grandparents, has said it at some point.

And that's because having a strong connection with our Self is fundamental to setting positive Conditions for our lives.

And yet many of us are uncertain of how to be true to ourselves. When asked to be that person, panic sets in. Being true to ourselves is about being genuine, true to our personality and to our character; it is about not being swayed by external pressures, not feeling we have to make a decision to be popular or fit in. This is often a hard task for leaders of organisations, who are bombarded with such pressures from staff, shareholders and customers nearly every minute of their working day.

The Self is essentially the authentic 'me'. It isn't really affected by external personality in any way, by who we are trying to become or how we act in the world; it is more about who we actually are. It's a level of us that is aware of ourselves and our motivations. The Self isn't really involved in doing much at all; it is much more about being. It's us without all the additional neurosis, anger, sadness and grief that we've lobbed on top of it.

Individuals with a strong sense of Self are essential to setting positive Conditions and are an essential part of any organisation.

If we have a strong sense of Self, we act as a Unifying Centre for the group or team we are leading. We know what we think and feel and are able to reflect on our experience. We are able to objectively observe ourselves, our behaviour and our decisions. We are a safe and reliable centre for our teams or for the organisation as a whole. Without individuals with a strong sense of Self leading a team, we have found within our own organisation that teams fracture, form cliques and ultimately fail.

Definition of the Self

'The self ... that is to say the point of pure awareness, is often confused with the conscious personality, but in reality is quite different from it. This can be ascertained by the use of careful introspection. The changing contents of our consciousness (the sensations, thoughts, feelings etc.) are one thing, while the "I" the "Self" the centre of our consciousness is another. From a certain point of view this difference can be compared to that existing between the white lighted area on a screen and the various pictures that are projected upon it ...

But the "man on the street" and even many well educated people do not take the trouble to observe themselves and discriminate; they drift on the surface of the mind stream and identify themselves with its successive waves, with the changing contents of their consciousness.'

Assagioli (2000)

The Values Universe model gives individuals a structure to develop and connect to their own sense of Self through the recognition of the Unifying Principles. By being aware of the Unifying Principles, decisions that are more considered and grounded will come about; decisions which aren't about the whim of the moment.

The Self has extraordinary potential which can be curtailed without appropriate reflection. By recognising and listening to our Root Needs, and answering them, we further develop the Unifying Principles. This has the potential to unify different parts of us and give us greater access to the Self. If we're unaware of them, we can create barriers. And the greater the sense of Self, the more we work on it, the more we create positive Conditions in our lives and in our teams, so our organisations become more unified.

The Will

With a strong sense of Self comes our Will. The two are intimately connected.

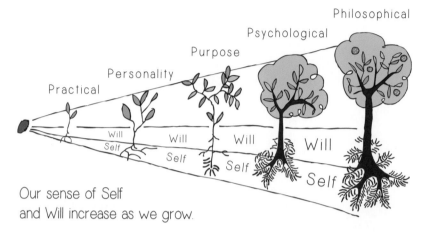

Our sense of Self and Will increase as we grow.

The Will is the part of the psyche that consciously galvanises us and motivates our actions. There are many acts of pure Will. Some people take cold showers daily. Sport enthusiasts spend hours on the same routine in the gym to achieve strength or fitness. Boxers train for months to win one fight. We recognise the capability of the Will most often in the physical achievements of athletes and explorers, and wherever there is an acknowledgement of having to do things that will cause discomfort in order to achieve goals.

Assagioli (2000) suggests that the first stage of training the Will is to recognise that each of us has one. In fact, he holds the view that for many people the Will has become lazy and disengaged and that this is the cause of many mental health problems.

So it can be with our organisations. The Will of an organisation and the individuals within it can be lost if there is a not a clear purpose rooted in Universal Values which engages and motivates those within it. If a genuine purpose is lacking, it becomes difficult to engage the Will except in short-term bursts, usually involving the promise of financial reward or promotion.

It is really important that the Will remains connected to our sense of Self and to the Universal Values that shape us. Without these connections, distortions can and will occur. Our purpose and focus become misdirected. We still have the Will to act, but our actions become less true to our authentic selves and to the values we hold dear. In short, we risk doing anything to achieve our goal – even if it is ultimately to the detriment of ourselves or to those around us.

Think of the athlete who relies on performance enhancing drugs, the leader who removes civil liberties to stay in control of his country at all costs and the organisation that is all about making money and doesn't care about its people or customers. The Will to do something is obviously still present – in fact, it's a dominant force – but gone are the connections to the Self and Universal Values.

Self-awareness reveals the mountains; with our Will we climb them.

So we see how a strong sense of Self and Will is a key part of setting the right Conditions.

A really good example of the power of the Will was the amazing feat accomplished by the comedian Eddie Izzard. In 2009, he turned up to his doctors only five weeks before he was due to start a series of 43 marathons back-to-back over 51 days with only one day off per week.

When his doctor asked him when he last ran a marathon, his answer was, 'Never!' When the doctor then asked him about his training, he said that he hadn't trained, and when the doctor finally asked him when he last exercised, Eddie said, 'At school!'

The doctor asked with incredulity what made him think that he could possibly achieve his goal. Eddie's answer was, 'I have decided to.'

He ran from London to Cardiff, Belfast, Edinburgh and back to London. He completed the last run on 15 September 2009 in the fastest time, after having run at least 27 miles each day, six days a week, for seven weeks straight, covering more than 1,100 miles.

And indeed at the time of writing he's at it again, running marathons in honour of Nelson Mandela in South Africa!

Mindfulness

Mindfulness has been described as 'bringing one's complete attention to the present experience on a moment-to-moment basis' (Marlatt & Kristeller, 1999) and as 'paying attention in a particular way: on purpose, in the present moment, and non-judgmentally' (Kabat-Zinn, 1994). We believe that mindfulness leads to a wisdom that comes from an awareness of the Self and of others; without it we act according to the whim of the moment.

But surely business is most often about action and not about sitting around all day being reflective?

Throughout history we have wanted our leaders to take action but also to be self-aware, because otherwise their actions might put us in danger as they make poor decisions based on their own neuroses, preferences or fears. We need our leaders to be mature, reflective people.

By being mindful it's easier to think about what Conditions we are setting up for ourselves and our lives. Mindfulness is practical; it focuses on and includes us, our motivation, our interaction and the world. It is about being still with an internal stillness, rather than a physical one.

"Mindfulness gives you time. Time gives you choices."

Bhante Henepola Gunaratana

Being mindful has to start with our current state, an awareness of interdependence and understanding how we can influence the Conditions in our lives.

Mindfulness

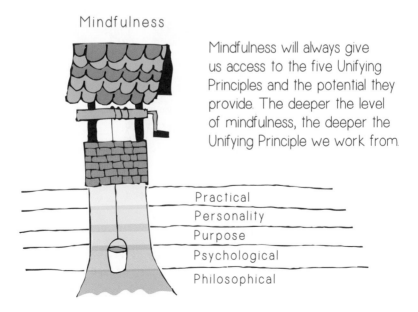

Mindfulness will always give us access to the five Unifying Principles and the potential they provide. The deeper the level of mindfulness, the deeper the Unifying Principle we work from.

Practical
Personality
Purpose
Psychological
Philosophical

The risk of shortcuts

Some modern management schools of thought use forms of Positive Mental Attitude which advocate ignoring or exchanging our emotional or mental states for preferred ones. The problem with this is that it can lead to frustration and disassociation. Advocates of these schools of thought will set their goals and then edit and replace any thought, feeling or behaviour of theirs that doesn't serve the attaining of their ends. It means we don't see ourselves as part of the answer or recognise our influence, power and role in setting Conditions. We believe we can change things without any work, action or effort. This then can offer a view of the world distorted by our obsession with getting something quickly, easily and for nothing. There's little encouragement to consider why we

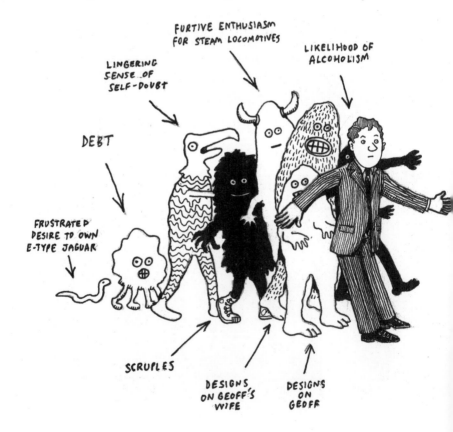

FURTIVE ENTHUSIASM
FOR STEAM LOCOMOTIVES

LIKELIHOOD OF
ALCOHOLISM

LINGERING
SENSE OF
SELF-DOUBT

DEBT

FRUSTRATED
DESIRE TO OWN
E-TYPE JAGUAR

SCRUPLES

DESIGNS
ON GEOFF'S
WIFE

DESIGNS
ON
GEOFF

are the way we are and what makes us do the things we do. We are asked only to envisage the world as we *want* it to be; an idealised vision of the future with us at the centre.

The bottom line is that avoidance, lying to ourselves, anything that we try and dump, hide or ignore, will come back to haunt us. It sits there suppressed and repressed, biding its time in our unconscious, just waiting for the slightest opportunity to rebel.

This will not only be the case for us as individuals, but also in our companies. Unethical decisions, cultures of blame, leading through manipulation and power, or even general laziness, ultimately will all come back to haunt us. For organisations are like individuals: abiding by the same rules and setting the same sorts of Conditions.

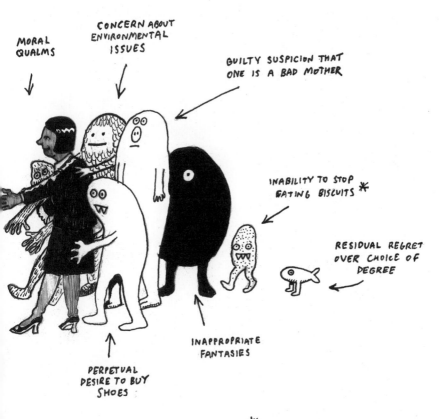

Organisations

As leaders it's our responsibility to be aware of Conditions within our organisations and how we might influence them. As the quote from Oscar Wilde at the start of this chapter succinctly states, when appropriate Conditions are set we are more likely to get the results we're looking to achieve. Without these, the intended results will be thrown off course or distorted. But whilst Wilde compares success to a science, our organisations are not laboratories and we cannot always control or manipulate all the variables that will impact on them. Neither would we want to.

Even individuals and organisations with good intent can set the wrong Conditions; it's not as straightforward as we might like to think. We can all fall into patterns of behaviour we are unaware of. Our own mental states, for better or for worse, set the Conditions for other people. When someone has got out of bed on the wrong side, their mood, actions and behaviour – if not recognised and held in check – can set the Conditions not only for that day but for the resulting relationships and decisions that are made on that day. And when Conditions are ignored or misdirected, distortions and degeneration take hold of individuals and groups.

Mindfulness and an acknowledgement of our interdependence are essential to avoiding this.

The Conditions within an organisation are multi-layered; they are not just about one person – everything is interdependent. From the physical environment to the mental and emotional states of the people within it, from the Conditions we can control, to those that we can't, all influence outcomes.

How we relate to and understand all the different subpersonalities in us will have a massive effect on the Conditions we set in our organisations. In groups, as with ourselves, our subpersonalities can distort and even take over. The dictator, saboteur or critic in the room can soon undermine any motivation or creativity, causing splitting and disharmony.

If the Unifying Principle needed is not modelled clearly enough by the leaders in our organisations then the subpersonalities of those in it can run riot. Having developed the Unifying Principle needed as leaders we bring what is missing. The group becomes less reactive and more able to stay with a clarity of intention and move forward.

Other factors that set Conditions for an organisation include the industry it operates in, and employee and customer perception. Even our competitors and their standards, our clients and their expectations, and our organisation's history, play a part. But more influential are the Conditions that we set and how we respond to these external factors. Universal Values and Unifying Principles set a framework for how we can give a considered response rather than a more acute reaction and will enable us to be more in tune with the Conditions we are setting.

Leaders are encouraged to become more aware and conscious of any existing, destructive patterns within themselves and their organisations and turn them into constructive patterns. These patterns will directly impact on the Conditions set.

When we walk into a meeting with our colleagues we don't start from scratch – we have a history which will massively influence our success. The history of the other people in the room, the history of the team itself – whether this is one of focus or bad habits – are both pre-existing Conditions which influence results.

For example, if as leaders we constantly leave unpleasant behaviour unchallenged, then we are very quickly setting up new Conditions for ourselves and our organisations. How often do we find ourselves talking about a fellow employee when the conversation moves from the professional to the personal? Of course, if this is to reinforce what a decent person they are, then great. But what a toxic environment we can create by talking badly of them behind their back. How great would it be to work somewhere – an organisation with Universal Values as its foundation – where those around you were critical to your face if they felt it necessary and yet found ways to praise you behind your back?

Leaders need to ask the obvious questions, and be mindful:

e Where do I sit within our organisation?

f What is my purpose?

▲ Am I a manager who needs to understand the Conditions at play within a team or department?

⫯ Or am I a Director or CEO whose concern is for the whole organisation?

- How much time do I spend on the practical day-to-day activities of my role, and am I lost in it?

- How much time as a manager do I spend on follow-up with my teams?

- Do I know enough about what's going on in order to follow up effectively?

- Does the amount of praise and recognition I give genuinely motivate or merely encourage complacency and a 'fat cat' mentality?

Praising inappropriately can be as harmful as ignoring or being harsh to staff, and only serves to re-set poor Conditions. Why might this be my tendency? Do I want to be liked more than respected? Of course, we understand that to some degree we may all want to be liked – but as senior managers it cannot be to the detriment of the team or the organisation as a whole.

"Teach us to care and not to care

Teach us to sit still."

T.S. Eliot

Setting Conditions – Higgs, Hadron and the Big Bang.

The ultimate in setting Conditions would be setting the Conditions for the origins of the universe.

The Large Hadron Collider near Geneva tries to recreate the Conditions in the universe just micro-seconds after the Big Bang. Hadrons are composite particles like protons and neutrons. The particle the team at CERN (that's French for the 'European Organisation for Nuclear Research') are especially keen to spot is the Higgs Boson. On 4 July 2012, two experiments announced they had each observed a new particle, although they still have a very long way to go.

Built by CERN, the Collider is a highly complex machine – a 3.8-metre-wide concrete-lined tunnel with a circumference of 27 kilometres, over 1,600 superconducting magnets each weighing around 27 tonnes (that's about 3 buses) and around 96 tonnes of liquid helium keeping the magnets cool. Its construction involved the collaboration of over 10,000 scientists and engineers from over 100 countries.

So if you think setting Conditions in your organisation is tough, just remember the team at CERN and the challenges they face trying to recreate the Conditions just after the Big Bang!

Dysfunctional organisations

Dysfunctional organisations are like dysfunctional minds. As the eminent psychotherapist Vera Vasarhelyi stated in conversation on 22 August 2012:

'The model for dysfunctional organisations is comparable with a state of depression in the individual.'

With this thought in mind, consider some of the symptoms of depression within an individual (NHS, 2014) and how these might apply to an organisation if the right Conditions are not set:

e loss of interest in things which used to be enjoyed
 lethargy
 finding it difficult to make decisions
e feeling irritable and intolerant of others.

Sound familiar? The main difference between individuals and organisations, of course, is that symptoms of depression may not always be within the control of individuals. A recent trauma, grief or loss, even the side effects of some prescribed medications, may bring on symptoms of individual depression. Whilst the activity of some organisations can of course be affected by economic climate and the like, there is much that an organisation can do to control its own Conditions, as we will explore.

Now consider the more extreme symptoms of psychopathy, now referred to as Anti-Social Personality Disorder. The symptoms listed are detailed on the NHS website (2014):

e The exploitation, manipulation or violation of the rights of others
 flattery and charm for own ends or personal profit
 being consistently irresponsible
 an inability to plan ahead
 a lack of concern or remorse about other people's distress
 irresponsible behaviour
 a lack of guilt and refusal to learn from mistakes.

We can all probably think of organisations that display at least some of these symptoms.

So, it's important that we ask the right questions, face our experiences and learn from them, be open and aware and not look for quick fixes, but really pay attention and pave the way for self-aware leaders and responsible organisations.

But how do we know what Conditions to set? How do we make sure we don't end up trying to control everything that crosses our path?

Sure, we can be aware of our interdependence and the Conditions we are setting up for ourselves and teams. But *just* being aware is not enough.

As leaders we need to know where to place our effort. How do we know what's missing and what we have in abundance? How do we see what is there in front of us and start to work on these existing Conditions to make a difference?

Our Values Universe model uses the five Unifying Principles to enable us to consider these questions and so set up the right Conditions for the Self to have a space to reflect and grow in the workplace.

Later in the book, we will explore the complexity of these Unifying Principles and precisely what they are because, whilst they are a key part of setting healthy Conditions, they can only take place in individuals and within organisations that have a connection with their Universal Values and a Philosophy.

And it is this aspect of setting Conditions that we will explore in the next chapter.

A story from Neil ...

Mindful Living
... or the lack of it.

I'd been sparring that morning. I felt tired, but good. I often felt like this after training, as though I was a bit more present, mindful and relaxed from all the exercise. The discipline was good for me.

The boxing gym was at the top of Railton Road in Brixton, known as the Frontline.

In the 1980s, and later when I was living there, the Frontline was the source of the Brixton riots. Both the community and police had felt a growing animosity to one another going back years. There was tension and conflict over everything from street trading without licences to cannabis smoking. In the community's opinion each was dealt with too harshly. Every interaction was setting the conditions for the next, elevating the distrust and anger on both sides. Most of the offences appeared to be minor, but the responses to them led to assumptions of institutionalised racism in the police.

Eventually, after a series of cannabis busts on the Frontline when some people got badly hurt, the touchpaper was lit. Brixton burst into flames.

The riot went on for three days.

Many individuals and small business owners wanted the police to intervene, including my uncle who owned the Esso garage at the corner of Coldharbour Lane, right in the middle of it all.

But they didn't.

Despite the impression given by the riots, Brixton in the 80s was full of life, colour, vibrancy and community. It was a fantastic mix of West Indian music, art and culture with British style and eccentricity. It was a good bus ride away from where I grew up, but my friends and I loved it. There were many areas like this in South London but Brixton was the best.

By the late 90s, Brixton had changed. Considerably harder drugs had been one of the big drivers. Things were not quite as I remembered.

In many ways the conditions set by the riots and the questions around racism in the police led to problems later. Brixton found itself with fewer police. From a feeling of heavy-handedness we were now left with light-touch policing, or so it seemed to those of us that lived there.

Gangs were more common, making claim to different parts of the streets. It was still full of characters and life, but more edgy, more dangerous.

One of these gangs had unfortunately pitched up at the end of my road.

As I approached with my short hair and largish frame, the leader of the gang stood up from the wall he'd been resting on and wandered up to me. I was tired after five hours of training and just wanted to get home. I stepped into the road to avoid any aggravation. But I had a feeling that I was in for some.

I was right.

The gang leader stepped up and blocked my path.

'Get off my yard,' he said.

'Your what?' I replied.

'My yard,' he said.

'If you can tell me where your yard starts and stops, I'll avoid it. But I live here. This is my road.' My intention wasn't to make a counter-claim to the road. I didn't intend to turn the conversation into a land dispute.

My enquiries about the boundaries involved didn't seem to make him happy. He became angrier and more menacing, so I turned away and gave him and his gang the widest berth possible. As I walked away he shouted for me to turn around. When I did, he pulled out his gun.

I never felt he was going to shoot me, but still …

This wasn't turning out to be a great day.

I got home pretty tired. I lay in my bath and read Carl Jung's Memories, Dreams and Reflections. I wondered if I could have done anything differently to avoid conflict in the street, but concluded I couldn't. I was relieved to be at home and not to have to deal with them again. At least not today.

It was about 4.30 in the afternoon.

When I got out the bath I needed to eat, then put out the rubbish for the next day's collection.

Not wanting to wear my towel to take the rubbish out, I searched for some clothes. There was one pair of pants left in my drawer - old boxer shorts bought for me years previously for my 18th birthday by my pal's older sister and her mates; they were fairly distinctive, with a large picture of male genitals on the front. These would have to do. They were a bit tight to say the least but looked a bit like shorts from a distance. Tight ones.

Still feeling a bit spaced out from my adventures earlier, I picked up the bags and walked them down four flights of stairs. I didn't need the keys, I could leave my apartment door open and run downstairs with the bags. Then all I needed to do was throw the bags at the pile of rubbish and run back upstairs. I opened the front door to the building, prepared to chuck the bags outside, but then I noticed they'd changed the rubbish area to a big metal bin.

What should I do?

I could throw the bags and let someone else put them in the new container. But that wasn't very considerate. I could go back up and put some dirty clothes on from the laundry, but I'd just had a bath. Alternatively, I could chance it and in ten seconds be back in the safety of the building. I grabbed the bags and dashed outside.

A massive gust of wind hit me as it swept along the road. I dropped the bags in the big bin and turned around to see, in painful slow motion, the large door slam shut with a bang. I felt the thud of it in the pit of my stomach.

My first thoughts were: 'I'm stuck outside, it will be dark in an hour or two and I have these embarrassing pants on.'

I ran to the door and shoulder-checked it in a state of panic, hoping against hope that somehow it would miraculously spring open.

Of course, it didn't.

I buzzed all the neighbours in the building but being late afternoon it was unlikely that there would be anyone home until around seven ish, maybe even later.

The panic started to grow in me as I realised the gravity of my situation.

I decided the next step would be to break back into my flat. I looked at the drainpipes that went up the side of my building to see if any went close to my half-open window on the top floor. There was one, but it was probably 35 feet up and at 14½ stone and six feet tall (actually I am 5' 11½ to my great annoyance) who knows if it would hold my weight.

As much as I was panicking, I didn't want to die.

'Okay, what are my other options here?' I thought.

I couldn't really knock on neighbours' doors. After all, it was the middle of Brixton and knocking on a stranger's door in only a tight pair of pants was probably not the best of ideas. I imagined them looking out of their window to see me standing on their doorstep trying to look like a man who had clothes on, carrying a briefcase.

This was clearly out.

Option number two, then:

I could really go at the front door repeatedly - shoulder-barge it until it broke. But I didn't want to draw attention from a neighbour who might then report to the police that a man in a pair of very tight pants with his genitals exposed was trying to barge his way into somebody's house.

Option number three:

Walk from here past the guys that threatened to shoot me earlier, down the Frontline and past all the good folk returning from their day's work, past the market where the unsuspecting people of Brixton were buying their veg and on to the fire station in the heart of Brixton. Then ring on their bell and suffer the subsequent shame, as clearly hilarity would break out amongst whoever answered and all their mates. I would then have to sit in the fire truck whilst they broke back into my flat.

And, of course, manage all of this without getting arrested or shot ...

Gritting my teeth and burying my shame somewhere deep in the unconscious, I picked my head up, tried to blank everything out and started to jog along my road barefoot in my pants to the fire station, about a mile away.

As I got the first ten yards into my jog, fear had a grip on me. To my horror, the gang were still there.

What if they thought I was some kind of nutter? That I had gone home angered by their attempt to bully me; that I'd been pacing my flat for the last hour thinking up a suitable revenge, eventually winding myself up into such a frenzy that I had run into my bedroom, put my tight fighting pants on, and prepared to charge them, death or glory style.

They would then shoot me.

I needed to calm down.

As I got closer, each one started to notice me, pointing me out to the others. Their reactions were a combination of laughter and mild concern. I was clearly a lunatic and, therefore, not to be trusted. By the time the ringleader saw that it was me running back along the street, that I was the guy they had recently had an altercation with, he was finding it so funny that the idea of pulling his gun again probably seemed to be a rude interruption of a good joke ...

I was clearly insane and most likely harmless.

I charged on barefoot down Railton Road, past the commuters, with my head held high, as though I did this every day in the same attire.

Having nothing on but pants didn't stop a local guy from trying to beg money from me.

'Where the hell does he think I'm keeping my wallet?' I thought.

'No mate. I'm in a rush,' I said.

For some reason this seemed to spur him on. With utter focus and determination, he sprang to life and started to jog next to me. Did he think I was doing this for charity or had some great mission to jog around the world in tight-fitting boxer shorts? Maybe he thought I was on a spiritual mission and he wanted to be my first follower ...

We silently jogged together along the busy road.

This was very tricky, as I had no shoes on; my biggest concern was to avoid glass or anything that might cause me an injury.

Eventually we hit the market, where my new friend soon got distracted and started begging others for cash.

People around me were so preoccupied with the price of fruit and veg that they barely noticed this nearly naked, barefooted man jogging past them.

Maybe they thought I had a pants stall and this was my way of publicising my new range.

Finally I reached the far end of the market and saw my destination ahead of me. Never before or since has a single building held so much promise and fear for me in the same moment.

I reached up and rang the bell with my heart thumping in my ears. Then slowly the shutter at the front of the station began to rise, creaking and rattling as it went.

Even before it was fully open a tide of laughter came from the dim station interior. My eyes became accustomed to the difference in light and I saw 20 blokes falling about in fits of laughter. I stood there feeling about 12 years old. I was numb, so to this day I don't remember all the jokes, questions and general hilarity that followed.

To top it all off, after they'd agreed to help me out and suited themselves up, they dropped a bombshell: they were going in the engine but I would have to jog back home. They took great pleasure in citing health and safety regulations. Nor did they offer to lend me any clothes. Why spoil a good joke?

'What doesn't kill you makes you stronger,' I thought, as I got back into my flat and jumped once again into the bath.

So what did I learn? Other than never go anywhere without your keys, particularly when you are half naked - which, to be fair, though good advice isn't particularly relevant to the Values Universe model. Well, perhaps it's this: that if we are considered, thoughtful and mindful and take into account the consequences of our decisions in each moment, rather than responding and reacting to situations as if we are in a constant state of emergency and panic, the Conditions that we set for ourselves may just be that much more constructive - and a lot less stressful.

"The moment you give up your principles and your values, you are **dead,** your culture is **dead,** your civilisation is **dead.**
Period."

Oriana Fallaci

VALUES AND PHILOSOPHY

Bringing ourselves to work

Many people don't like to bring themselves to work. People hold back part of themselves because they don't want to give the bit that's really them, their authentic self, to their work.

In many ways, our personality has to either take a back seat or shrink to fit the organisation we work for.

The most successful organisations galvanise the values inherent within the workforce. And yet there is an irony at play, because our sense and expression of values appears to have shrunk more to our personal and private space rather than something we naturally think about at work.

We think that's a mistake.

In a survey by the World Economic Forum conducted in December 2009 and published in 2010, the majority of people do not consider that they apply the same values in their private and professional lives. In the same survey, honesty, integrity and transparency are the most important values according to 51% of all respondents. More than two-thirds of respondents believe the global economic crisis is also a crisis of ethics and values.

We have discovered that keeping back a part of us from work – far from *saving the best bit of us* for our friends and family, pastimes and outside interests – has the reverse effect. We end up leading fragmented lives, dissatisfied and frustrated. We spend vast amounts of energy keeping that part separate. Effectively we break off large and small bits of ourselves, and then play a specific role depending on the context we're in. We adopt the role of the employee or the party-goer, the parent or the sports team member. We are never fully ourselves.

Do any of us really want to work in an organisation where we feel we can't be ourselves? We may be successful, we may be able to section ourselves off, but it's a fragmented way to live and takes a lot of emotional and physical energy. We're role-playing according to the context we're in.

The importance of authenticity

We believe it's important that people are encouraged not to 'fake it', not to 'play' at being an employee or to act out a fantasy projection of the kind of employee they believe the company wants them to be. Of course, we all fulfil roles in all kinds of ways, but there are authentic and inauthentic ways of doing that.

'Authenticity' is the extent to which we are true to our own personality, spirit or character despite external pressures.

Authenticity develops when we are genuine; when our behaviour and actions stem from who we are and not what other people want or expect us to be. We can be who we are wherever we are, someone who is not to be defined by a list of expected behaviours to 'fit in'; someone who is setting positive Conditions for ourselves and for others. 'Bringing ourselves to work' and being 'authentic' does not mean, however, we can become 'unedited' in the workplace.

Missed bus

Breakfast argument with Mrs Jenkins about toast

Refused membership of golf club

Just as the environment cultivates openness, it should also encourage maturity and mindfulness. What can really help us be ourselves at work is if the values we are asked to adopt at work correspond to the values – the Universal Values – that we believe we all share.

Defining values – the difference between Universal and Cultural Values

To understand the Values Universe we must first explore what we mean by values. We recognise that there are many different definitions and interpretations of values in philosophy, sociology, theology, politics and other disciplines, and it is not our intention to start competing with Socrates, Locke, Mills or Marx or any other influential world thinkers. No. For us the most important distinctions are between what we define as Universal Values and Cultural Values.

Universal Values exist within us as core human values that almost all of us want to live by: honesty, empathy, compassion, non-violence, love and tolerance. They enable us to build healthy relationships both with ourselves and with others and underpin all positive and thriving groups, communities and organisations. They cannot be dreamed up and imposed upon us by over-zealous bosses or CEOs. They don't isolate or exclude; by their very nature they are all-embracing.

But we don't always live by these deep positive values because, especially in business and at work, we think they might *just get in the way.* Let's be honest, none of us have to look far to see evidence of individuals who seem to be highly successful in business, finances and in relationships who couldn't care less about values. Some people may argue that they are not an essential ingredient for success, but our ideas take as their foundation that life is so much better when we do work to these Universal Values.

Indifference to Universal Values can be catastrophic. Wars, famine, poverty, abuse, murder and violence would be unchecked without a moral and ethical frame of reference. In business, too, the impact of indifference can be huge.

There are countless situations in the UK alone where decision-making in business has paid little regard to Universal Values, such as the fixing of the LIBOR or the *News of the World* journalists who illegally hacked phone messages. Add to this the MPs who claimed expenses they weren't entitled to, the failures of management and care which led to deaths at Mid Staffordshire Hospital, and the scandal of horse meat finding its way into some beefburgers and ready meals.

Layered onto our Universal Values are our Cultural Values. These are the values we can be most unconscious of.

Without a doubt, our Cultural Values are important to us as individuals, defining who we are and where we come from.

They are an essential ingredient in the rich tapestry that makes up the myriad of different societies across our planet. However, they also have the potential to distort Universal Values to meet the needs of the cultural grouping in which they have evolved.

The Greek philosopher Plato recognised this, and went so far as to say that values only matter when they are Universal and beyond self-interest. Universal Values, for Plato, are central to human development and fundamental to physical, emotional and spiritual well-being.

There are certainly risks attached to prioritising Cultural Values over Universal Values; when not kept in check, we can begin to exclude, judge and even harm others.

But our own approach recognises that both sets of values co-exist and as such both matter.

Whilst many, like Plato, may argue for a world that prizes only Universal Values over the more self-interested Cultural Values, this is not only unrealistic but also damaging to our humanity. After all, it would be inauthentic as human beings to suppress all that makes us 'us' – and Cultural Values are a valuable part of that, provided, of course, they don't become barriers.

Our model therefore seeks to encourage and embrace individual differences whilst placing greatest emphasis on Universal Values. The fact is we should *celebrate* our Cultural Values and *act* according to Universal Values – that way, everyone's beliefs and cultures are accepted. At a time when some people in society feel their culture and the values associated with it are being eroded, that they cannot be their authentic selves unless they are in an environment with those of the same culture, it is important that we recognise how important Universal Values are. When we act according to these, all cultures and individuals are embraced, welcomed and given permission to be their authentic selves.

What is important is the way that the group treats its members, reacts to situations, pulls together when things get tough and welcomes, accepts and values people new to the organisation – because all these will be influenced by how much the group has internalised and prioritised Universal Values over Cultural ones. It will be a fundamental part of the organisation's Conditions and will enable those within it to thrive; there will be less chance of cultural cliques, groups within groups and rivalry developing.

- Where do you see cliques in your organisation?

- What pay-off is there for the members?

- Are you part of a clique?

- What Conditions exist to support the continued existence of these cliques?

- What is it that connects or unites the individual members?

- What unrecognised or unresolved issues might have set the Conditions for these cliques to form and thrive?

- Consider ways in which you might re-set these Conditions.

Where there is any strong, well-established cultural grouping, there is always the risk that that group may not always be respectful or welcoming to outsiders. Whether consciously or not, it may be perceived as hostile or even tribal to those who are not a part of it.

Cultural Values

Cultural Values tend to be internalised during our upbringing, often absorbed from our parents and siblings without realising it – nationality, ethnicity, religion, politics, how we hold our knife and fork (or chopsticks), the TV programmes we watch, newspapers or websites we read or teams we support, our prejudices, stereotypes and assumptions.

Cultural Values deeply influence what foods to eat, the clothes we buy, who to marry or shun. Some may stem from religion; some may arise in times of war, others in peace time. Some people may see them as a direct gift from their given deity, others as the pragmatic solution to communal living.

The workplace can foster this kind of thinking. None of us has to go far back into our work history to remember when we were the outsider, or made to feel separate, different or small. The fear of going to work can be felt as strongly as the fear we may have felt as a child going to school. And, in the same way that child psychologists recognise children can struggle to focus on school work when driven by high levels of anxiety, our performance at work can be similarly impaired.

Anxiety is common to each and all of us, and necessary in measured amounts to keep us safe and focused. However, when worries, fears and anxieties become excessive or continue over a prolonged period, the effects can be debilitating. Whilst our natural 'fight, flight or freeze' response may help us avoid immediate danger or meet a deadline, the physical and psychological by-products of feeling under threat and 'primed for action' over a long period are at best uncomfortable and at worst incapacitating and unproductive – as the following graph shows (Dr Helen Kennerley, Clinical Psychologist, Oxford).

In terms of the workforce, the much-followed business innovator Dr Edwards Deming (1982) wrote:

'The economic loss from fear is appalling. It is necessary, for better quality and productivity, that people feel secure.'

This is why anxiety created by being an outsider at work or in a group can keep us from being fully present, because we have no investment in the aims and goals of a group, they do not concern us.

Eventually we may be accepted in. But if we go along with the 'favoured' cultural way of thinking, the group will behave as it always has. The Conditions will be left unchallenged.

Spot the clique

- Have you ever been excluded from a group or situation?

- Can you remember what it felt like?

- What behaviour did you observe in other people that led to you feeling that way?

- Have you ever excluded anyone from a group or situation – either at work or in your personal life?

- What were your reasons for doing so?

- How did it make you feel?

In an attempt to present an overwhelmingly positive image to the world, organisations can fall into the trap of prioritising Cultural Values at the expense of Universal Values. They can look to define a list of desired behaviours, qualities or personality traits that match their brand and the image they want to present to their customers.

It's not an unusual approach for organisations to take. Whether you sit within the service sector or your company hails from a different sector completely, listing out a desired set of traits or indeed a long list of values can be seen as essential to defining the ideal employee. Whilst at face value these traits may indeed create the desired customer experience, there is a subtle but vital difference between this approach and ours.

Any attempt to define traits will always be externally imposed rather than intrinsically felt by its staff members. Our approach is the internalisation of principles – what we refer to as the Unifying Principles – rather than adherence to an external idea of ideal behaviours. Doing this, we become less reliant on policing behaviours and instead develop the idea of recognising, habitualising, internalising and then modelling these Unifying Principles to others. Principles can be associated with the simple completion of tasks (Practical) or the modelling of good interpersonal skills (Personality), but the idea of internalising and then modelling is a subtle yet important divergence from the idea of externally imposed rules and requirements.

The attempt of many organisations to impose a list of desired traits or qualities demonstrates the growing commercial value of being human (or at least being perceived to be) in the workplace. But what happens when the manager isn't there checking behaviours? Do people revert to something else? Ultimately, in our opinion, this model doesn't feel very authentic. It is an attempt to turn certain Universal Values into a product, a commodity at the expense of our authentic selves. Feeling aligned to the Philosophy of a given organisation does not need to undermine individuality – despite many organisations misguidedly attempting to do just that.

'I've found you don't need to be a certain type of person, have a certain level of education or have had a certain type of upbringing to "fit in" at HOME. Everybody has the right to speak their mind and to ask questions, no matter what level they are at. This encourages open and honest debate across the company. Frank discussions happen when needed, but always in a friendly way, and we're encouraged not to talk behind each other's backs. All of this essentially helps us to become better people. Not many companies can say they do that for their staff!'

Lisa, Head of IT, HOME Fundraising

Values are not about image

At HOME we don't publish a specific list of Universal Values. We don't define them for our clients, refer to them on our website or have tailored training courses spouting the virtue of each individual one to new recruits.

That would be totally missing the point.

Why?

If we choose respect, empathy or honesty, does that then mean that we don't value kindness, sincerity or integrity? It would be odd to go on about respect being vital to our business but not really giving a damn about honesty, for instance.

The fact is that Universal Values can only be contained and given life in one's actions and behaviour; they come from an internal sense of what is important to us as human beings rather than from a need to impress.

- Can you think of an occasion when you went directly against your values?

- What made you do it?

- Was it external pressure to behave in a certain way? Or did it come from a conscious internal decision that you made independently?

- What were the consequences of the behaviour – for you or for others?

- How did it leave you feeling?

- Would you make the same decision again?

Moving beyond values

So, right about now, we imagine you've got a pretty good understanding of the differences between Universal and Cultural Values, and the importance of respecting both whilst putting an emphasis on the Universal if your organisation is to be successful and authentic. 'But how', you might be asking, 'do I begin to put all this into practice?'

The point is, Universal Values by themselves are not enough. They are elements in our Values Universe but, like any universe, they are governed by natural laws that provide a framework to hold them together. That framework in our model comes from the recognition in us and our organisations of the five Unifying Principles. At its core a company needs something to ground it, to give it direction and meaning. As with individuals, companies also need a Philosophy.

A Philosophy is the first step in communicating your values.

An organisation should set a Philosophy to provide meaning to what we are doing; something that people can engage with and connect to. The skill is in creating a Philosophy that respects who we are and can include our own sense of meaning. We can then include ourselves more deeply.

Establishing our own Philosophy

After a few years in business we faced the dilemma of many young companies: whether to expand or consolidate. Demand from customers was growing along with our reputation. There were natural economic benefits to scaling up our operations as well. But we were keenly aware of the dangers of growing for growth's sake and the risk of compromising the reputation for quality that we had established in our formative years.

As senior managers we had practical knowledge and skill, but we had also recognised that there was something deeper – other reasons why staff, clients and stakeholders were interested in our company and increasingly loyal.

Despite the diversity of the many individuals that made up our company, what brought us together and kept us together was our sense of Universal Values.

And it was these values that translated into the following Philosophy, which continues to underpin everything we do to this day:

❧ to make a positive difference to the world/be a positive influence on the world

➤ to be successful

➤ to be better people.

In defining our Philosophy, we had found a way to articulate in a simple, direct way the shared Universal Values that were already binding us together. Many commercial branding exercises begin by defining what values underpin the company, are apparent in its activities and products and are shared by its stakeholders.

A proposition and a Philosophy is then written based on these values. The mistake is that the organisations often don't differentiate (and don't see the difference) between Universal and Cultural Values, and then attempt to imprint the mantras of the corporate belief system as propaganda and dogma – rather than by connecting the Philosophy to the fundamental Universal Values we all share, and by leaders setting good examples for others.

For us, everything starts and ends with the Universal Values within our organisation, and our Philosophy is an expression of this.

One way to gauge the values of your organisation is to play the following game.

Consider a scenario where the Daleks have just successfully conquered your country and have set up a puppet government. Which values in your organisation would be held by collaborators, which would inspire resistance?

Whether visible or invisible, accidental or by design, your organisation, too, will have a set of values, Philosophy and Unifying Principles that reach out to and influence every person and function within it. This is happening now in every single organisation out there – some with good effects and some with bad, for where there are people there are values. The choice is only about making them conscious or not.

The type of organisation you have and the state it's in will determine whether you as a leadership team want to define the Philosophy exclusively or whether you consult and involve others in the organisation. It is not essential to involve everyone in setting the organisation's Philosophy. As we elaborate on Unifying Principles, leadership and influence later in the book, you'll appreciate why.

Remember you are establishing more than a mission statement to sell to clients or shareholders; it is the cornerstone running through your organisation. This will be internalised and modelled by everyone in every action. It doesn't have to sound clever. It just has to be true.

HOME's Philosophy reflects our belief that people have great potential and are at their best when they are themselves. Too many organisations employ people and then wish to modify them, to make them fit a corporate 'norm' and to somehow 'average' them as people.

We don't.

This is borne out by the variety of people and characters we have in our organisation: their backgrounds, beliefs, education, class, personality traits – even their fashion preferences. Unlike some organisations, we don't recruit on the basis of hair style or colour, regional accent or ability to stay jolly all the time. We're interested in the human being behind all of that. There is never the sense within our organisation that you have to be a certain type of person to do a particular role or develop and progress in the company. We don't limit people with our definitions of who we think they are or where they might best fit within the organisation.

Having a strong sense of the Philosophy running through the company, and it being clearly communicated by its leaders, means that there's a gravitational pull helping to align all actions and decisions with that Philosophy.

In the early stages of our development at HOME, we certainly recognised the influence our Philosophy was having over the practical application of what we were able to achieve as a company (in our case fundraising).

Defining your own personal philosophy

Let's forget about organisations for the moment.

If you had to define your own personal philosophy, what would it look like?

Write down three key statements that would be at the heart of it; include the Universal Values that are already important to you.

Remember: your philosophy underpins everything that you do – how you act, the decisions you make, what you do, what you don't do. It defines how you live your life.

How distortions can occur

However they manifest themselves, distortions will always show through, but they can be hard to spot. They can creep up on us and be present even when our intentions are honourable. The 'attractiveness' of our people and organisations on the outside will soon reflect any 'ugliness' that develops on the inside. In business terms this means brand degradation and loss of respect in employment markets and the marketplace itself; something no amount of 'rebranding' can fix. All this starts from the core of the organisation. By purely choosing values such as personal ambition, greed or a quest for power, the actions and behaviour of the group become distorted – destructive and damaging at the very least, and ultimately failing.

Reflect upon your own organisation. Are there any ways in which what is presented on the outside to customers or clients is quite different to what actually goes on within the organisation?

€ Why do you think this is?

ᵃ What purpose does it serve?

Now reflect upon yourself as an individual.

€ Are there any ways in which what you present to the outside world is quite different to what you think and feel internally?

€ Why do you think this is?

€ What purpose does this behaviour serve?

If, like Oscar Wilde's Dorian Gray, we are only concerned that our future actions make us look better to the outside world, there is a real danger our superficiality will show through.

All distorted value systems have the desire to control at their root and achieve this desire through a toxic mix of fear and greed. Fear and greed push us apart and isolate us, turning us against one another and triggering our survival instincts. Authoritarian control can be seen as the only way of keeping the group together.

An ethical product or service does not equal a strong philosophy.

Distortions occur if we put the type of work, the product or service above the Philosophy – even when that product or service is an ethical one. In fact, there is an assumption that because what an organisation is 'selling' is ethical, moral or for a good cause, its values and Philosophy are also ethical and moral.

Not true.

Organisations with ethical products can suffer from huge distortions. In many ways, the ethical nature of the product doesn't help, as the organisational culture doesn't feel the need to grow or mature. Instead, it becomes complacent and self-congratulating: 'The product is good; therefore we are good. It has values; therefore we must have values.' So, with this auto-destructive assumption, many organisations miss the opportunity to reach their full potential.

The sayings 'Greed is good' and 'If we don't do it then someone else will' may have been the way to convince Wall Street executives to become successful, but is this really the best individual and organisational outlook? Do we believe ourselves to be so separate from others that our actions will have little or no consequence?

Do we really not care?

We like to think that most people do.

Surely, the better way forward is to focus on what's best in us? The reality of motivating purely through fear, unchecked greed and ego-based power is that we fail to help our staff understand the link between emotional maturity and responsibility.

If greed is good, the greediest among us must become the most successful.

But when we look at our staff, we don't choose them for promotion by how unpleasant and greedy they are. We know that their effect will be more benign and, therefore, better generally if they display a good degree of emotional maturity. Indeed, people work for those that they believe to be decent and mature.

This, then, is as much about nurturing and developing the human side of us as it is about setting and meeting targets, because once we understand the link between *success* and *maturity of the individual*, we start to model these qualities to others as criteria for success.

Now, we can't vouch for what it feels like to work for Innocent Drinks, the company most famous for smoothies (perhaps if you do, you'd like to let us know), but they had a Philosophy we really liked the sound of – for all sorts of reasons. They set it out on their website (2012) like this:

'When we started Innocent 14 years ago, it was with the aim of doing business in a truly good way – to make products that taste good, that do people some good, and to do good in the wider world too. It hasn't always been easy, but having a set of clear and simple values has helped shape the business we've become.'

We liked it because: Innocent's Philosophy is simple and clearly communicated. Simplicity is reflected throughout all their communications – even down to product packaging. The Philosophy has people and the Universal Value of doing good at its heart. It's human. It attempts to make an emotional connection and doesn't just focus on the outcome, but more on the 'how'. There's substance behind it; it's not saying it wants to do one thing and then delivers another. We believe it. It's not trying to be clever for the sake of it. And its Philosophy is backed up by Innocent's products and underpinned by its values.

Take a look at their current website and see how they talk about themselves now. What do you think?

Engaging the Will of the group

In psychological terms, when a group is united through shared values and Philosophy and as a consequence is motivated to act together in a common aim, we say that the group's Will has been triggered and engaged.

But how do we begin to create a unified group with the Values Universe model? We first need a self-aware leader who models the Unifying Principles and so sets positive Conditions. This individual then becomes a Unifying Centre. He or she models and inspires belief in their own purpose and so brings purpose to the group.

When more staff Root Needs are met, their energy, commitment, creativity and focus also rise. One example of this within HOME is the payroll team, who consistently recognise the need to get it right. A real sense of purpose has been trained into and modelled to them by Michelle, the head of department. She explains the effect payroll has on other people – on their lives, on them as individuals and on their families. But it's not just in what she says; it's in what she models. Through her energy and commitment, everyone in her department sees and feels the knock-on effect and responsibility of what they do. When we had a new payroll system that had just been implemented and wasn't working as smoothly as it should have been, Omar, Earle and Sonya stayed up all night to input all the data manually and so ensure staff, suppliers and clients were paid on time. No one asked them to do it. They knew and felt the impact not getting it done would have on the individuals concerned. The strong sense of purpose had been brought to the group by its leader.

When we connect to Universal Values and a Philosophy as individuals, we come together to act. We see this when we look at how mass fundraising charity appeals have raised millions for famine relief or the victims of earthquakes and tsunamis.

Triggering the Will is the essence of motivation. It's what organisations around the world pay millions for – how to tap into and motivate the Will of their employees. Our model highlights the fact that motivation does not in the main come from external factors but from internal ones.

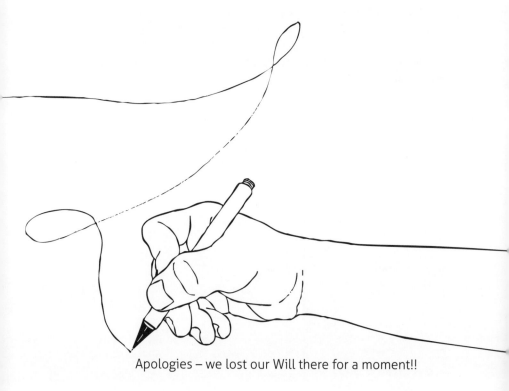

Apologies – we lost our Will there for a moment!!

For some reason, some organisations are convinced that if you place a dozen phrases in bullet points and project them on a screen, it turns a mediocre idea into a work of genius that will engage and motivate a whole team. Don't get us wrong – it can be a good communication tool, but too often is used as a replacement for serious thought and genuine engagement.

Have you ever been to such a presentation where someone complained that it was too short?

We thought not.

If you shine a list of values on a screen, they cannot magically transfuse into the audience. Rest assured it doesn't work, however dark the room and bright the bulb.

We know it's hard to believe, but some of the world's greatest philosophical and scientific breakthroughs were made without the benefit of PowerPoint.

If you want to know how corporate culture can deaden the spirit and take the passion out of a call to action, take a look at the corporate version of an extract from Churchill's famous speech set out below:

We shall fight:

	Yes or No	Risk Assessment
e on the beaches	◯ ◯	◯
ꜱ on the landing grounds	◯ ◯	◯
◣ in the fields	◯ ◯	◯
e in the streets	◯ ◯	◯
ꜰ in the hills	◯ ◯	◯
e we shall never surrender	◯ ◯	◯

When we are in charge of others, we have a responsibility to them. We see it as fundamental to the role of a board or senior management that they seek to understand themselves and others and act to support their team on their voyage. Once a leader takes the effort to understand, that effort becomes more and more worthwhile (as we'll show) in the way it touches and engages individuals and teams, in the way it inspires and encourages accomplishment and in the way it enhances performance, productivity, loyalty and buy-in.

And, ultimately, in the positive impact it has on the bottom line.

Many companies today emphasise how much fun there is to be had at work. Recreational facilities are now a sign of a considerate and affirming culture to motivate and encourage loyalty.

Of course, these facilities help and a lot of research has been done on the use of recreation in setting the right psychological Conditions to stimulate creativity and problem solving in the workforce. But we think that the fun should also come from being engaged in the task. This often stems from seeing the meaning in it. In other words, the work itself can provide the satisfaction.

For many people, work is a place of competition, a place to manipulate or be manipulated and where survival rests on ruthless action.

This is probably easy to understand; after all, we are a species of hunter-gatherers. The workplace can easily become a territory in which the instinct for survival rules. But this is not Ancient Rome or the Middle Ages, and we are not gladiators or serfs. Robert from accounts may have engaged his inner warrior at the company's paintballing weekend, but truly he ran little risk of actually dying in a hail of fluorescent acrylic.

If a person doesn't derive satisfaction from their role, if they are not engaged with and connected to the organisational Philosophy, then no number of table tennis or billiard tables will replace it.

JENKINS DOG WALKING SERVICE
RECREATION SUPER-HUB

Corporates are great at hiring people to inspire the workforce; people who have had near-death experiences or come through terrible hardships (often having played for England!). But being on the corporate after-dinner circuit is not really how anyone wants to end up after a medal – the food is generally poor and the hours antisocial.

If motivational speakers actually motivated, of course, you'd never need to invite them back or get another next year. No one says, 'Boy, I'm motivated now.' Everyone says 'Wow, what a great motivational speaker – he was amazing, get me another vodka.' Often they leave us with a slight sense of inadequacy or inability to relate escaping a burning destroyer or scoring a hat-trick to working in a call centre, where remarkably there are no air-to-sea missile attacks, goalposts or indeed anything that has a smack of adventure – only acres of people with headsets.

How many of your staff dread Monday morning and, if observed closely, appear to want to be anywhere rather than working? Indeed, via the internet or texting, they probably are elsewhere. Think of the hopes and motivations that are edited out of their workplace selves and how many in the company live for the weekend.

Let's return to the thinking of Maslow. This recognises that once our most basic and fundamental needs are met – food, water, shelter, etc. – we become aware of new 'higher' levels of needs that, once also met, reveal yet further, more refined needs.

We like to apply Maslow's thinking to an organisation's relationship with its people.

When we look at an advert for a job, we ask, 'Does it meet my basic needs for food, water, shelter and safety?' Yet countless studies have shown that, whilst this might get us interested, this is rarely the reason we stay with an organisation.

Developing a clear and authentic Philosophy at the heart of an organisation establishes it as a place where the Root Needs of its employees are met. People will feel valued, will want to stay and reinvest at greater depth, with more of themselves. The more an individual's Root Needs are met, the more they are able to give back. There's a direct connection between an organisation's success and the degree to which it meets the Root Needs of its members. Even on a basic level staff will stay longer, and so with them stays the training and expertise they have developed whilst with the organisation.

This is not to say that one shouldn't operate a series of firm policies or targets – far from it. We and our senior staff members remain extremely focused on the performance, outputs and outcomes of our company. But, that said, if the only driver to retaining a motivated stable workforce is money, the company and the people in it will be placed under huge financial pressure.

By communicating and embedding a Philosophy that connects to people's Root Needs and their Will, a deepening attachment to the organisation is stirred within each of us. Firstly, we have finally 'come home' in some way, to an organisation that shares our philosophical outlook and Universal Values, and secondly, because our Root Needs are met, we can develop and mature as individuals.

What exists now is not just a working environment filled with lots of highly motivated *individuals* all working hard, having their needs met, and wanting to stick around. What exists now is a highly-motivated *group*. This is the benefit of working with the Unifying Principles.

You may be thinking: 'This is all very well, but I work for the world's biggest manufacturer of non-plastic earplugs. How can I be inspired and motivated by that? My job is rubbish. I hate earplugs. I have nightmares about being chased by earplugs ...'

But, no matter how mundane the product or the service provided, you would certainly want to work for a company that had a clearly defined Philosophy and a real sense of its Universal Values, so that you are able to feel part of something and be engaged with its intentions on an emotional level.

One element of our own organisation's Philosophy is 'to be successful', but we don't say in what; we just say that we want people to be successful. Now success in our eyes might be becoming better people or doing good; it isn't necessarily all about making money, though of course we want our company and our people to do well financially. We leave it for the individual to interpret in their own way – to think how it might apply to them personally and professionally, how they can embed it into their day-to-day work and ensure they can be the best they can be, do what they do and do it well.

The idea of a good working Philosophy based on Universal rather than Cultural Values is that it can be deliberately broad. It's not always necessary to give the precise detail of what to do or how to do it. At HOME, our Philosophy reflects the spirit in which we manage our business and the desired outcomes of what we are doing. That's what includes people. We leave the door open to say, 'I want to be creative as well. I want to be successful. I want to help people in the world. I want to develop myself as a human being.'

But obviously there's a danger that a Philosophy is so broad it doesn't touch anyone or relate to anything. To just say, 'We want to be truly human' may sound overly idealistic. Time needs to be spent on getting this right – on being specific enough, whilst also remaining inclusive and Universal.

At HOME it would have been far easier, financially speaking, to set up a model whereby we used subcontractors to deliver our fundraising services in the field. However, we feel the best way to be true to our Philosophy is to employ all of our people directly, be 100% accountable for each and every one of them and take the financial risk in doing so. Obviously, there are different considerations and different risks for companies active in different sectors.

There are countless examples from the financial industry over the past decade where the decisions of senior executives have placed an emphasis on immediate gain over sustainability. Think of the disastrous impact at Lehman Brothers. With a massive growth in assets and turnover in the period leading up to the bank's demise in 2008, the Philosophy became hopelessly wed to a culture of short-termism which, as we know, caused ripple effects far beyond the company itself. An institution over 150 years old and the fourth largest investment bank in the USA was wiped out in a relatively short period due to a huge distortion of its Philosophy. A sobering thought.

Bankers have of course been much demonised, and yet do we really think the majority of the people working in the financial industry went into work with the intention of doing wrong? They are not the only organisations who put financial outcomes at the heart of their purpose. So what happens? How is it that our values can get distorted?

Sometimes nothing is what happens; inaction can be as harmful as action.

The fact is that when financial goals alone are at the centre of an organisation's Philosophy – whatever the organisation, whatever the industry sector – people will be encouraged to step on each other, all in the name of reaching that Philosophy.

And just for the record ...

Just because we're running closer to the breadline at times and things become tense, it doesn't mean that our values have to go out of the window. Actually our values, reinforced by the Unifying Principles, are what have kept us in business; they are the currency that has kept us going. They have meant that we could 'rally the troops' because people cared about the future of our organisation. People worked over and above what was expected – our Philosophy has ensured, however, that we don't take advantage of that.

Another story from Neil ...

Reg the dog

(or why values on their own just aren't enough)

My schooling, or lack of it, took place in a couple of different comprehensive schools around South London.

In the late 70s and early 80s, these were an interesting experience. Your first aim was to survive, and the second to keep any new clothes that may have been bought for you by your parents. You could always tell the tough kids. They were the ones wearing the same Harrington jacket or loafer shoes all year.

Teachers saw their jobs as crowd control. Learning seemed low on the list of priorities for teachers and pupils. In fact, in many cases, the teachers were bullied by the pupils.

I didn't excel. I left at 16 years old.

Everybody did.

After 18 months of badly paid jobs, I found myself involved in the world of business-to-business publishing. Riveting publications like *Reproduction* (alas, a printing title) and *Office Equipment News* had the great fortune of employing me as a Production Assistant. This involved checking artwork in and out ready for printing, drinking coffee and alcohol, and mucking about with colleagues in the print room. I wasn't very good but I was diligent. The people that I worked with were patient and took me under their wing.

After a couple of days it was clear that the company had many different departments all working to produce some of the elegant titles I refer to. One of those was the advertising sales team. They had company cars, expense accounts and came and went as they saw fit.

Even better, it became clear that they spent a large part of their time 'entertaining'.

'I can "entertain"', I thought.

Somehow, through constant badgering I managed to get a job selling display space in one of the magazines. It was just before my 18th birthday, and with this came my first company car, my first expense account and my first suit. Actually that last bit isn't true - I had a fantastic tonic suit during my cool period aged 11 to 14. The suit was brown fading into green - brilliant.

I was very young but very enthusiastic.

As I got into my new job, it soon became clear to me that the trick was not to have the best magazine; the trick was showing clients the best time.

This I could do ...

I soon used my talent to competitive advantage - taking clients not only to restaurants, pubs and parties, but finishing the evening in London's fashionable nightclubs, where I had friends working as doormen, so we were well looked after.

In a very short time I was getting big contracts and building a reputation as 'the chap to guarantee a good time'.

On the surface, of course, I looked very professional. I worked for good magazines and the client was getting good responses from the ads.

At 22, I had made it to the dizzy heights of Group Advertising Manager (GAM). I ran all the teams and ads on a few business-to-business titles. I was very young. By far the youngest GAM of the time - reached in the most part because publishing was incredibly incestuous and I was well-known for getting and keeping clients.

I wasn't a great salesman and frankly didn't have any interest in being one. I was, however, pretty good at showing clients a good time. Monday would arrive and the business would be mine.

But all this came at a cost.

I was out all week drinking, partying and falling out of clubs at 4am. I was waking up counting the minutes until my first drink.

I was tired - not in the normal way, although that was certainly part of it. But much more deeply. I was tired of myself.

Was this it? Was this what I offered the world?

The final epiphany happened with me standing on a desk at the office surrounded by ad men, shirt off (tie still on), shouting, 'Have you nothing better to be doing with your empty lives?!'

I was fired.

This period of introspection continued, as I realised that mine was the empty and shallow life.

I was determined to change. The old 'me' had gone. I was no longer this cocky man about town. I was instead a new man, reborn, out to save the world. I had a plan:

Step 1
Go vegetarian, read stuff, buy Joni Mitchell and Crosby Stills and Nash LPs.

Step 2
Learn to meditate and get my head together - guru up!

Step 3
Save humanity - and the environment (time permitting).

Step 1 was okay. Apart from the problem that almost nobody was vegetarian. There was a range of veggie sausages out but they were dangerous and could be used as a cosh in a tight spot. So in reality it just meant eating the same as others without the meat. Sunday dinner was potatoes, broccoli and carrots. Lunch was cheese sandwiches, etc.

I lost weight and gained hair.

Twice a week, I took a short bus ride to the Buddhist Centre in Croydon as per Step 2. Being slightly short-sighted I also invested in some John Lennon-type glasses. I had always avoided the wearing of glasses, as it meant getting punched a lot where I grew up. I wear them sometimes now and have what must be the fairly unique experience of feeling brave when doing so.

So now for Step 3. Who can I save?

As I got off the 154 bus, the answer presented itself in front of me.

A huge Golden Labrador seemed to be dragging itself along the edge of a front garden only a couple of yards from the main road. My heart sank. Clearly this poor animal had been hit by one of the many irresponsible drivers flying along the main road. In desperation he seemed to be dragging himself to the nearest safe space.

He looked unconcerned. 'Must be stunned from the blow of the car', I thought. 'I must get him to a vet.' But he was a BIG dog. No matter, I was fit and young, clearly the right man for the job. I picked him up, placed his front legs over my shoulder and started to walk down the road.

He stared at me with a puzzled look on his face as he rested upon my shoulder. On we went.

I had no plan. I just walked with this enormous dog staring at me constantly. It was more than 30 degrees, I was starting to sweat and my new John Lennon glasses kept falling off.

All of a sudden we were surrounded by children leaving a local junior school.

They seemed to gather round in their hundreds from nowhere.

'What's happened?' they asked.

I explained. Clearly the real story was about me and my heroism. The dog was now a bit player.

One of the mums offered me and my over-sized hairy companion a lift to her vets, only a couple of miles away. 'Maybe they can save him?' she said. 'Thank you very much,' I replied, relieved that I wouldn't have to carry him all the way.

The estate car was filled with children, all extremely concerned about the dog. I had to repeat the story over and over. Each time my part in it sounded strangely more heroic. There may have been a bit about me jumping off a moving bus and rescuing him from something ...

We arrived only just before the story became completely unrecognisable. On telling the story to the receptionist – the latest one where I am very heroic – she kindly rushed us in to see Mr Collins.

The dog lay there staring at us all, looking baffled by the events of the day.

'Yep,' said the vet, 'he seems to have lost all functioning in the back half of his body. This is probably the result of an accident.'

Immediately I grabbed one more opportunity to tell my heroic tale. 'I would agree with your theory about being hit by a motorist if it wasn't for the fact that he doesn't look like he's in any pain.'

I explained that I put that down to him being in a state of shock. 'Mmmm, maybe ...' he said. 'What can you do for him?' I asked.

'Well, I can send him off for X-rays and let you know in a few days ... OR PUT HIM DOWN RIGHT NOW.'

My heart sank. There was a pause whilst the vet and the woman and all the children stared at me, waiting for an answer ...

What! How did I get myself into this dilemma? Was it always going to be like this, saving things in general? If I said to put him down, I would have to try and track the owner down and tell them.

My mind was flooded with anxiety, but I needed to live up to my new flares.

'No' I said. 'Please don't. Are there no other options?'

'Well, you can find the owner and let them decide, if you feel more comfortable with that. Try starting with the police. Someone may have reported him missing.'

Within minutes we were back in the car making our way to the local police station.

I ran inside with my new four-legged friend whilst my entourage waited outside.

'Has anyone reported a Golden Labrador missing?' I said, turning sideways so that the duty officer had a good look at the dog's features. As if a Golden Labrador wasn't enough and that his face would be the decisive factor in the whole recognition (e.g. yes, we have a Golden Labrador reported missing, but not with such penetrating eyes).

'No,' said the duty officer, 'no dogs reported missing, golden or otherwise.'

'We can put him down if you want. We can call a vet in.'

'No,' I said.

'Well, you need to find the owner, then,' he said. 'Try going back to the place where you found him.'

I picked up my hairy, confused friend and made my way back to the car.

'We have to go,' the woman said. 'Can we drop the two of you anywhere?'

'Is there any chance of taking us back to the road I found him in?' I said. 'Maybe I'll ask around, see if anyone is missing a Labrador.'

As I sat in the car, comments about his smell were now overtaking the concern.

The options so far were rubbish:

1) Have him put down.

2) Find the owner, then probably have him put down.

As we approached the place that I first saved him, I saw an old man and his dog. I shouted out of the window of the car, 'Excuse me mate. You know this dog?'

The old man slowly leaned into the car. 'Reg,' he said, 'Yes, I know him. He's got dodgy back legs, ain't he? Drags them about when he walks. Can't move far really; only a few feet.'

My heart leaped into my mouth. I felt sick. My John Lennon glasses steamed up.

My mind struggled hard to NOT put together all this information. But the harder I tried not to, the faster I made all the connections.

Reg had clearly been left in the front garden by his loving owner to enjoy the sunshine and watch the world go by peacefully. There would be no worry about him running off, as they had done this a thousand times before. Even in the most extreme circumstances he could only go a couple of feet anyway, and loved sitting watching the people and cars go by until some raving hairy lunatic in a ridiculous pair of glasses and embarrassing jeans kidnaps him and nearly has him murdered ... twice.

I froze as the car drove off towards our final destination.

For all but me this new information was a reason for celebration. There was excitement in the car, as nobody had yet realised I actually found him in his own front garden. As we pulled around the corner, all my worst fears were made manifest. We could see four or five people chatting with neighbours and looking up and down the road, clearly concerned.

The car pulled up 50 yards short and the woman and her children and their friends all got out and ran to the small group of people to deliver the good news.

'Goodbye, Reg,' I said. 'Sorry about that.'

I jumped out of the car and ran with all my might, flares crashing around my shins, glasses steaming up, and disappeared down an alley to safety ...

So, amidst my humiliation, what did I learn?

Values are not a pick'n'mix selection where we choose the most interesting ones, the ones that sound impressive or inspiring or those which fit with a particular image we'd like to portray to the outside world. Neither are they about random, isolated acts of heroism or being a 'good' person. Values are not just about our view of the world, our attitudes and our behaviours, despite how important these may be. Values are about outcomes. Measurable outcomes. Outcomes that at the very least avoid the pointless killing of an arthritic labrador.

NO DOGS WERE INJURED IN THE PRODUCTION OF THIS BOOK

"**Change** your opinions,
KEEP to your **principles;**
change your **Leaves,**
keep intact your **roots."**

Victor Hugo

UNIFYING PRINCIPLES, LEADERSHIP AND INFLUENCE

Recognising human needs

At root, we are driven to be as much ourselves as we can be in the world. Just as a tree in the Amazon will grow hundreds of feet, pushing up to the high canopy to access sunlight, so we have a need to grow in the world, to influence our environment, to interact with it and make sense of it in one way or another. Not only to access more resources or attention, like the Amazonian tree, but because we crave as much life as we can possibly live in one lifetime.

On a day-to-day 'conscious' level our motivation can feel foggy, a mix of various wants and needs all looking to get met through the activities we involve ourselves in. We might think that the drive to get out of bed and involve ourselves in the day is motivated by external influences such as attraction, fear and status. 'I like this, therefore I'll do it; I want that, so I'll do this to get it; I'm worried about this outcome, so I won't do that ...' and so on.

The problem with this is that before long we can find our lives lacking direction and substance. We are buffeted along on the currents of fortune and forces seemingly outside our control. We then start to look internally for something to make sense of our experience, and to give it shape, narrative and purpose. We are filled with a series of questions:

What are our real needs (Root Needs, as we call them) and what are mere wants? Or which needs are archetypal – needs that form the foundation of our being – and which are ancillary, transitory, mere whims of the moment, insignificant in the grand scheme of our lives? These are important questions to address, so we know what Conditions we are setting up to meet those needs.

In his hierarchy, Maslow talks about the need for water, food, shelter, respect and self-awareness. Clearly these are all vital to us throughout our journey in the world. After all, like the tree in the Amazon, we can't focus on becoming fully manifest if we aren't sustained by our environment. Survival naturally comes before full manifestation.

But in Maslow's terms it is only at the pinnacle of the hierarchy that we experience internal needs, the sort that relate more fully to the deeper parts of us. It's as though we can wait until all the other needs are met, prioritising ourselves down the list until we have engineered a structure in which to house ourselves.

We have a huge amount of respect for Maslow, but we differ on this point. In our view, it is only through meeting and developing ourselves internally that we provide a sustainable response to our external needs. Internally we find resources that engage us, inspire us, drive us. By meeting our Root Needs, we can tackle our problems and lead ourselves to internal and external growth. Through meeting internal needs we set the Conditions for continued internal growth and greater external manifestation.

A history of needs and callings

The idea of the deeper parts of us sending messages out like beacons to our conscious mind, messages that cannot be ignored, is far from new.

The Ancient Greek poets depicted these needs or callings from the unconscious as encounters with the gods. The god would appear, often in disguise, to deliver a message that would change the course the hero was taking and get them back on track. The notion of ignoring the call of the gods was unthinkable and would ultimately result in shame, madness, destruction, and even death.

And this is not just true of Classical literature; it is also part of myth and legend from all across the globe. They were ideas that continued to appear later with the Romantics and the Pre-Raphaelites, ideas that were ultimately adopted and explored in other fields of study, including psychology and anthropology.

At the popular end of anthropology, the hero's journey as explored by Joseph Campbell in *The Hero with a Thousand Faces* (1949) argues that in myths and tales the hero has no choice but to listen to the call from within. Once they listen and accept the call, they undertake a quest into the unconscious – often represented by a strange land with different 'rules' – in order to retrieve lost, buried or stolen treasures or elixirs which, once won, are brought back to the people in order to heal them: first the calling or need, then the journey full of pitfalls and obstacles, then the pay-off.

Of course these symbolic stories externalise the pay-off as an object of great power, beauty or significance. But the real story or end result is that the voyage leads to us gaining more of our deeper humanity.

More recently, in *The Soul's Code* (1997) James Hillman, like Jung, talks about these needs as a calling and recognises that for centuries different cultures, religions, philosophers and creative minds have searched for the right term for the source of this 'call':

'The Romans named it your genius; the Greeks your daimon; and the Christians your guardian angel. The Romantics, like Keats, said the call came from the heart ...'

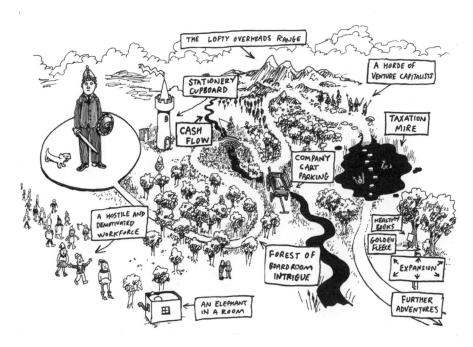

Hillman also recognises that 'a calling may be postponed, avoided, intermittently missed. It may also possess you completely. Whatever; eventually it will out. It makes its claim.'

Now, just to be clear here, we're not saying that our managers and leaders are all heroes on some kind of mystical journey, or that they should be pencilling in regular 'quest meetings' to discuss the recapture of long-lost treasure or go around healing themselves and others – we admit that all sounds a little overblown.

But, whether we're aware of it or not, the search for humanity does go on in our workplace. It doesn't just stop at the reception desk – or certainly it shouldn't. We don't have to go through some kind of security scanner where we are searched for any trace of humanity, which needs to be removed for the safety of others before entering the workplace.

But, in many ways, at its very heart business creation is a hero's journey of sorts.

Our view of needs: Root Needs

Hillman and others often focus on the call or need as part of a search for deep meaning. We take this further and recognise that there isn't just one need but a series of five Root Needs that ask to be listened to and are an essential part of the development of our whole character and psyche.

Far from just giving us meaning, we see the meeting of our Root Needs as providing us with a series of stepping stones that enable us to develop a broad spectrum of character traits that we and others can see, feel and rely on. Certainly meaning is one of them, but practical skills, identity, purpose and psychological wholeness are just as important in their own way.

So whilst we're not the first to talk about needs, we are perhaps the first to talk about them in the context of reaching our full potential in every respect.

Needs and callings in life tend to be associated with religious or spiritual experiences – as though only a deep and profound experience will break through from the unconscious and make a demand for expression and change. We believe that all of the Root Needs have value and are part of developing our whole being – that a search for deep meaning or a spiritual journey of some kind is no more important than the search for identity or purpose; they are equally important roads that need to be walked. The meeting of each of our Root Needs seeks to make us more alive, more manifest, more authentically us on every level.

These Root Needs are in us as individuals and therefore also within our groups and organisations. They represent different parts of ourselves that have to be integrated into the whole of us in order for the psyche to mature. They ask us to make sense of who we are and why we are here.

The Root Needs are:

- the **practical** need to *do*

- the need to have a strong identity – our **personality**

- the need to understand our place in the world, our **purpose** and where we're going

- the **psychological** need to be whole

- and the need for deeper **philosophical** meaning.

The journey through these five landscapes has long-lasting benefits. We listen to ourselves, to what we genuinely need, and act on it. We change our course and take ourselves in the direction we actually need to go in, and so we trigger our Will. This is an experience we probably all recognise when we feel that something in our life needs to change. It could manifest as a call for a career change or a radically different direction in education; it could be taking up an art; it could result in seeking out more supportive company or letting go of destructive relationships. The ways these calls for growth and change are experienced are as varied as we are. And at first we may resist these changes, as they can mean upheaval. But often by accepting them – by listening to the need – we can feel more energetic and more complete.

We can sometimes spend a vast amount of energy in life subconsciously resisting the things that will actually do us the most good. There can be any number of reasons for this, ranging from complex emotional issues that may require unpicking, to a more general fear of change; fear that we will have to stop doing things the way we normally do them and take the risk of trying something new. It's common. We all do it to some degree or another. We feel the internal pressure that builds up when we fail to respond, and rather than address the problem we bury it, blot it out, distract ourselves, purposefully get caught up in something that's far more 'important', something far more pressing and compelling or far less risky. And so we move a step further away from being more authentic.

To correct this, we have to slow down, take some time to reflect and become more mindful. We have to be prepared not only to listen to our Root Needs, but to respond and act on them too and so unify around them. It is at this point that we start to develop our character and become more manifest and present in the world.

When we meet our Root Needs, everything changes; not only our relationship with ourselves but also in the groups we run and in our natural ability to lead. Over many years and in many different arenas, we have observed how meeting the Root Needs develops, strengthens and grows parts of us. For us, this isn't something theoretical but a tangible, observable phenomenon that we've seen in thousands of groups of different sizes in different scenarios. When we meet the Root Needs, the rest of us feels more unified. Previous concerns, wants and needs can seem trivial, as we feel more grounded, present and part of our life.

Meeting Root Needs through Unifying Principles

The Root Needs are calling to us: 'Make me part of your life!' They are calls to grow and develop our psyches so we have more Self and Will in our lives. The Self is the origin of that call – you'll remember from our earlier definition that it is our 'point of pure awareness ... the centre of consciousness' (Assagioli, 2000).

The Unifying Principles provide us with a way for us to be true to ourselves, for the psyche to grow and mature – and to do so safely in stages. We have developed a system that allows us to transform gradually and gently over time. This makes it sustainable, not a quick fix. It's a process of evolution rather than an attempt at a 'smash and grab' on the Self.

Through the Unifying Principles we take it one step at a time, enabling each one to bed in before we move on. We condition our minds over time to assimilate new ways of being. So we set firmer foundations for our success.

We see this play out time and time again when teaching meditation. When people start practising they often experience incredible gains almost immediately, like they've suddenly switched to a super-food diet or put a high-performance engine in their old car. But often these gains are short-lived, as they are unable to sustain this new 'power' they have access to. Often this results in students of meditation giving up their practice prematurely.

Our response to the call of the Root Needs at various stages in our life creates the chapter headings of our life story and gives shape to the narrative of our lives. They are like archetypal stages we all pass through as we develop and mature.

So in early life we experience the need to *do*. This can be seen as the drive to be distinct in our environment. Then we begin to look for our identity, seen most clearly through our teenage years right into our twenties, the need for purpose then arising a few years later and so on.

Sometimes we can get stuck in these stages and find it hard to move on. We probably all know adults who seem to behave like children or teenagers and people who are still struggling to find their own identity.

The benefits of working to the Values Universe model are that we don't have to wait for the Root Needs to emerge shouting and screaming for attention at a particular stage in our lives. Neither do we have to be stuck at one particular stage of our lives for years without any method of moving forward or satisfying this Root Need.

Through the Unifying Principles, we can build places for meeting the needs in our lives at any point. This means that a 25 year old working to the Values Universe could model more mindfulness, wisdom and awareness than a 70 year old who has not done any work on their self-development. And certainly we see this played out time and time again within our own organisation, where people in their twenties are mindful and respected leaders.

As we respond to the Root Needs step by step through the Unifying Principles, we also change our view of life as we change the lens through which we look at it.

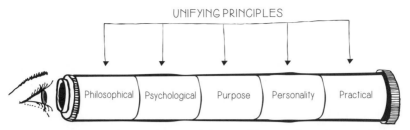

UNIFYING PRINCIPLES

| Philosophical | Psychological | Purpose | Personality | Practical |

If we see ourselves, others and the world around us through the Unifying Principles, we see differently

When the Unifying Principles are at play, we gain lasting character benefits and attributes that we can trust in and return to time and time again.

Essentially the Unifying Principles come about as a part of a natural process. They develop within us in response to the Root Needs we have recognised. They are active parts of the psyche around which we unify – and so have already been going on in us to some degree all our lives. But by being more conscious of them, we can develop the Unifying Principles even more. When we recognise the needs and bring them into our consciousness through the Unifying Principles, we change how we relate to ourselves and to others. As we then unify these parts of us, we naturally have a unifying effect on the groups we run.

If the leader of a group has met their own Root Needs, the individuals within the group will unify around the leader. This is because the leader will be modelling the Principle back to the group, highlighting the Root Need that we all have. When these Root Needs are not recognised and not modelled back to the group through the Unifying Principles, then the group can become distorted in many ways, falling into destructive or Will-less states.

Steps in developing and forming the Unifying Principles

The first stage in the development of the Unifying Principles is that we recognise we have Root Needs which call to us to be more manifest in the world.

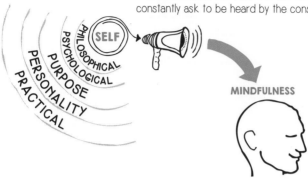

I. Need

The Root Needs from the Self are ever present and constantly ask to be heard by the conscious mind

In order for us to 'tune in' to our Root Needs, we have to employ mindfulness. This is supported by a knowledge of the Root Needs as a guide to direct our awareness. If we know what the Root Needs are, we have something to apply mindfulness to – so if we lack Purpose, applying mindfulness to examining why we've made some of the big choices in life will help us understand what's missing.

I. Need

The Root Needs from the Self are ever present and constantly ask to be heard by the conscious mind

MINDFULNESS

2. Mindfulness

Through mindfulness we hear our needs

??? What is it I need?

Through mindfulness we deepen our understanding

MINDFULNESS

We respond to our Root Needs, thus reinforcing and developing our corresponding Unifying Principles. Responding to the Root Need for identity strengthens the Personality Principle, for example. The more fully we meet the Need, the more 'substance' we give to the Unifying Principle. It helps to think of the Unifying Principles as something that are built through responding to the Root Need, like building a bridge between everyday consciousness and the Self.

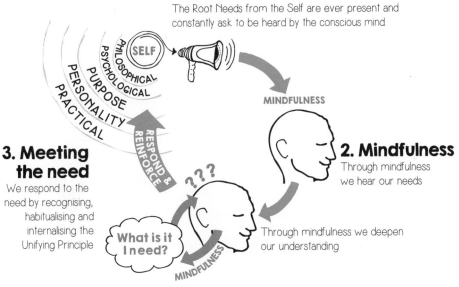

I. Need
The Root Needs from the Self are ever present and constantly ask to be heard by the conscious mind

MINDFULNESS

3. Meeting the need
We respond to the need by recognising, habitualising and internalising the Unifying Principle

What is it I need?

2. Mindfulness
Through mindfulness we hear our needs

Through mindfulness we deepen our understanding

The more fully we respond, the more sturdy the bridge becomes, allowing us to get closer to the Self – but also allowing the Self and Will to get closer to us. So the Unifying Principles are like muscles – the more we use them, the stronger they become, and the more our Root Needs are answered.

If our leaders cannot listen and respond to their own needs, then they will not develop or mature; their organisations and teams will suffer if not supported at deeper levels.

Without mindfulness and listening to these needs, leaders will not offer a Unifying Centre for the group.

Groups and the individuals within them will not function for long without the 'centres' the Unifying Principles provide, because a strong, solid core is crucial for a healthy team culture with a strong sense of Self and an active Will.

Modelling is a process by which one person serves as a model for others by embodying deeper parts of the character that they trigger in others. It is often an unconscious communication.

If the Root Needs of the individual and the organisation as a whole are to be met, as leaders we need to bring the Unifying Principles to the group; to *recognise, habitualise, internalise and model* each of the Unifying Principles.

If the people leading us do not satisfy these Root Needs, others will step in to take up the mantle – others who may not share our values or Philosophy, and may model negative distortions as positive.

When we recognise, habitualise and internalise, the trust in our abilities grows and our influence becomes greater.

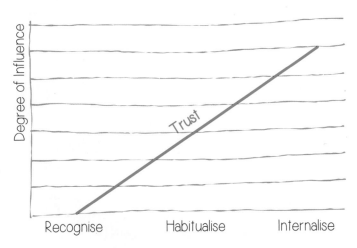

Key stages from recognition of the Root Need, to modelling the Unifying Principle:

Recognise: through mindfulness we identify the Root Need on a conscious level. Remember the spectrum of needs runs from the need to *do* (the Practical) through to the need for a greater sense of meaning (the Philosophical).

Habitualise: we remain aware of the need and practise taking the steps to meet it through our actions. This becomes a regular habit.

Internalise: the Unifying Principle is at play. Listening to and meeting the need is so much our habit, it becomes second nature and is in tune with our Self. As our Will is triggered, the gains now become obvious to us.

Model: the gains of the Unifying Principle become more obvious to those around us. We model it to others and begin to trigger the Will of the group.

Once we have internalised, we naturally model to and influence those around us; we have a positive impact on Conditions.

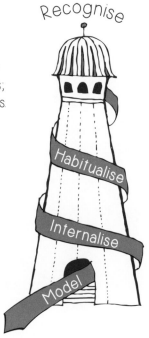

Internalising the Unifying Principles

Over the years, we have noticed that people habitualise and internalise in various ways at different levels.

Think of martial arts. You start off with a white or yellow belt and work hard to make your way through the different coloured belts to black or beyond.

At black belt you don't throw away what you've learned in the previous levels. At each and every stage you are required to practise, integrate and build on the skills you have learned from the previous level. Without this, you cannot progress. Your techniques and understanding of the principles behind these gradually deepen and become more and more internalised and your practice becomes stronger and more effective. This is the case for quantum physics, sailing, glass blowing, managing and leading organisations. It's true for almost everything we do in life.

The more we practise and internalise the Unifying Principles, the more they become part of us, the stronger and more effective we become. We model them at a deeper level and so have more influence on the groups we lead as they begin to recognise, habitualise and internalise the Unifying Principles for themselves and then trigger them in other people.

Entering the zone

For any athlete and coach, the zone is the optimum, where body and mind function automatically, reacting to the challenges of the moment.

Dr Larry W. Judge describes the flow state as 'an experience athletes get wherein everything they do seems effortless. Within the state of flow is a delicate balance between skill level and challenge. If the demands of an activity are greater than one's skills, then a state of anxiety is a result. If the skill level exceeds the situational challenges, boredom will result. A flow state includes the achievement of a positive state void of either of these conditions. The participants allow themselves to be athletes and surrender their subconscious minds to "auto pilot". In this state, athletes produce their best performances'. (Judge, 2010)

Obviously this isn't just applicable to athletes. We all have moments when we relinquish conscious control and have fully internalised the task at hand – although Dom has experienced a distortion of this concept and come perilously close to losing any form of consciousness when sharing the boxing ring with Neil on one or two occasions! Consequently Dom yearns for a return fixture on the judo mat. Not that he's bitter. No!

To recap, the five Unifying Principles are the:

- Practical Principle
- Personality Principle
- Purpose Principle
- Psychological Principle
- Philosophical Principle

As we've mentioned, we all experience these Unifying Principles to some extent. They have been going on in us and the people around us all our lives, because self-realisation, development and growth are a part of life. Some of us will have developed them more than others, but no one is starting from scratch because these Principles are innate.

Let's explore them one by one.

Practical Principle

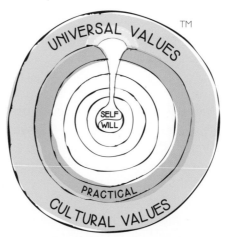

The Practical Principle develops when we recognise the Root Need to *do* and we respond to it. The need to *do* is primal – it's the need to have an effect, to show we exist and to have our existence reflected back at us through our environment. Without the basics at this level we are unable to grow to meet other needs or to engage the other Unifying Principles – or indeed to survive.

We can recognise, habitualise and internalise any process leading to practical output – be it the maintenance of machines, balancing the numbers on a balance sheet or perfecting our golf swing.

Any learned process, if we do it enough, eventually becomes habit and, for us to become better and more successful – or simply maintain good performance – it's helpful to understand how each practical action influences the next: if we do X, we will achieve Y.

> "... to learn and not to do is really not to learn. To know and not to do is really not to know."
>
> Stephen Covey

Practice makes pathways

'Every move that we make, every thought, sense, emotion, perception or idea involves the firing, or excitation of neural pathways ...' (Hudson-Allez, 2009)

If this neural activity can make the appropriate connections in our brain, it lays down shortcuts or 'neural pathways', which it protects for ease of subsequent use with a fatty substance called myelin. 'The easy use of pre-prepared pathways allows individuals to learn routines of behaviour that make life quick and easy for us.' (Hudson-Allez, 2009)

And this process continues throughout our lives. Contrary to popular wisdom, 'old dogs' can indeed be taught 'new tricks'. Recent developments in neuroscience are proving that the brain's plasticity does not cease around the age of 14 years as previously thought, but continues over our lifetime.

However, just as these neural shortcuts make life easier, they can get in the way. Where learned behaviours are no longer useful to us, they can impede our development rather than enhance it. We therefore need to remain mindful of which of our default ways of being remain useful and which no longer serve us well.

Like a child learning to walk or to tie their shoelaces, in an organisation it's the basics of the Practical Principle we have to recognise, habitualise and internalise before we can work towards any of the other Unifying Principles.

Its development shows through in our ability to link one task with another. For example, when we learn to cross a road there are basic lessons we learn about crossing all roads. We don't need to start again for every road that we cross. When mindful of working to the Practical Principle, we develop common sense. We can make the link between the doing of one thing and the doing of another.

A highly developed Practical Principle

Possibly the perfect example of someone displaying a strong Practical Principle is adventurer, writer and television presenter Edward Michael 'Bear' Grylls.

We may know Grylls from television shows like *Man vs. Wild* in which he strands himself in remote locations to demonstrate the application of survival skills he's internalised.

Some might argue that Grylls is able to survive extreme conditions thanks to his knowledge and training. We would argue that it is a highly developed Practical Principle that enables Grylls to absorb and apply that training and to be creative with his knowledge, applying the Principles he's learned in one situation to similar situations.

Without the Practical Principle at work, Grylls would have situation-specific skills that he would have to re-learn each and every time he was dropped into a dangerous situation. Or, to put it another way, without the Practical Principle 'Bear' Grylls would cease to be!

As we are conscious of the Root Need to *do*, the Will develops naturally. We also get confidence and self-belief. We trust ourselves with more tasks, we can relax, and with this comes more ability to be in the moment. We are meeting the Root Need. We are unifying ourselves around the Principle we have gained.

By being mindful of the Practical Principle, we learn efficiency, so less effort is wasted. We learn how to follow and stick to the steps that each task demands. It helps us to apply cognitive thought to each task and enables us to develop an understanding of how our output influences our lives and the group around us, and benefits the organisation as a whole.

When fundraisers join our company, we introduce them to the six steps approach. This is one of the tools we have designed and developed to support staff at the Practical level, to teach them the fundamental aspects of fundraising ethically and effectively.

Colleagues may show a new recruit a method for a task which will certainly save a great deal of time. However, the internalising of the task, making it a habit and then second nature, can only be done by the new recruit, no matter how good the teaching is.

They must recognise, habitualise and internalise the task until they orientate themselves around the Practical Principle. For example, someone can explain and show us how to ride a bike, but it is only we who can actually learn how to ride it; only then can we get the feel of it and internalise it.

As leaders we always model the Practical Principle to others. It is the first level at which our staff buy into us because in many respects the practical aspects of our jobs are the most visible to others, and the ones that initially indicate how capable we are. We don't necessarily have to be an expert in the same fields as all our staff, but we do need to have a strong awareness and practical skills in the area that we are responsible for – even if that is simply *managing the team.*

As a Unifying Principle, the Practical level may be the most basic but it is also the most fundamental. Without it we can't get anywhere; we receive little respect from our teams or colleagues around us.

Distortions at the level of the Practical Principle

Whatever the Unifying Principle we are working from, distortions occur when we fail to recognise the need, or fail to respond to it appropriately – usually because we haven't referred to Universal Values or are only acting with self-interest.

A distortion of the Practical Principle is not to see the links between things. For example, a member of the team may need to be shown each component part of an individual task on multiple occasions, rather than habitualising and internalising the skill through experience.

The ultimate distortion of the Practical Principle might be to opt out of doing altogether; to 'learn helplessness' as a way of passing on the need to do. Because the need to *do* is so fundamental to us, when we lose touch with it, for whatever reason, the consequences can be pretty devastating. We are no longer getting feedback from the world outside or inside and so we can feel Will-less, or we could be full of Will but with no way to express it constructively.

When the Practical Principle in an organisation goes awry, the business will survive at best, fail at worst; it will not succeed. Many mediocre businesses tick over where the Practical Principle is distorted, it's true. We see organisations out there surviving with masses of people doing things badly just because they have a monopoly of sorts. We have all used them. But isn't it a painful, unpleasant, energy-draining process dealing with them? If every business failed where the Practical Principle went awry, in some ways it would be marvellous because the only businesses that survived would be those that are really well run. Think of all the hours of our lives we would save.

Principles build character,
distortions undermine it.

If we want to develop a good reputation as a business, we are absolutely reliant on people performing the Practical elements of their roles. In common with many employers, we have found over the years that a number of employees have been unable to get to grips with the Practical Principle in their role. This has taken up endless management time where the supervisor has found themselves drawn into a world of constant explanation and re-iteration. Clearly we give people the time and support to develop, but it is only when an individual has habitualised their practical role that they start to really benefit the organisation.

It is when things are not right at this level that people are most often fired, as the individual cannot respond to the Practical Needs of the organisation – they cannot *do*.

However, no matter how highly developed, the Practical Principle doesn't address the depth of our commitment to the task or how much we care about outcomes. Eventually we reach the limits of its effectiveness, as there is not the ability to unify other parts of us and therefore the group around it. If the group makes the Practical task the primary focus without an awareness of the other Unifying Principles and their importance, then the group will not unify. For example, we all experience a need to develop a sense of our own identity. We want this to be recognised by others, we want to work with others, to collaborate. For this we need to unify around the Personality Principle.

The greater the Practical Principle in individuals, the greater the Practical Principle in the organisation.

Create in your mind the picture of an individual who only focuses on the Practical Principle. Make some notes if that helps. What would it be like to be them, to work with them, to be their friend?

Now imagine the kind of company they'd create. What would it be like if they were running it? How would it treat people? What would it be like to work there? What would the customer experience be like?

Now have a think about how you might focus too much on the Practical Principle. Where might it cause problems for you and those you work with?

Personality Principle

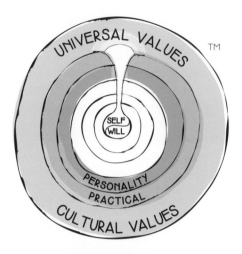

The Personality Principle develops when we recognise the Root Need for identity and respond to it.

Of course, many forms of philosophy and psychology are testament to the early need for a strong sense of identity; to have a strong connection to our interpersonal world; to discover what we feel, think or like and what we don't.

'For most people, all of life is a period of growth and development, experimenting and testing, searching through trial and error for harmonious ways to allow the intrapsychic structure of the real self to express itself in the physical world through relationships and work.' (Masterson, 1988)

With the Personality Principle we bring our own personal uniqueness and integrity to Practical tasks as well as our need for relationships. It's all about our ability to express, interact and co-operate, listen to and understand ourselves and others in interpersonal and social situations. It's about knowing what we feel and being able to communicate it to others effectively. It's also about how we demonstrate empathy through our ability to listen and consider another person's perspective.

By being mindful we learn to trust the Personality Principle, and we can relax a bit. We don't have to try to invent an 'us' in every emerging situation. We can rely instead upon our ability to respond authentically and be ourselves.

Sometimes there is a risk that our sense of Self can disappear when we are anxious, especially when in unfamiliar situations. Maybe there are situations that require us to be chatty or interactive when we are naturally shy and so find them difficult. We can feel as though we have to be 'someone else' to survive them.

"Those who wish to **transform the world** must be able to transform themselves"

Konrad Heiden

In fact, our strength lies not in our ability to cover up or manipulate ourselves or others, but to be true to ourselves; to relax a bit and give ourselves a break.

When the Personality Principle is triggered, we lay Conditions for healthy, honest relationships by unifying the interpersonal – our emotions, thoughts, feelings, what we want, what we don't want, what we like and what we don't like. We will bring personality traits such as empathy, kindness – and the odd distortion, too, such as a desire to fit in or be top dog – and these factors will shape our experience and how others experience us.

Think about how a small team operates. The leader of the group must find ways to motivate the collective Will of the group, to meet targets and deadlines. In a small group they will use their own Personality to do this.

Their own ability to know what they feel and think, as well as the ability to empathise and listen, will inform their success. Individual connections will be made and habits generated that get the group to fulfil its mission.

Distortions and the 'false self'

'Like other creatures whose early survival is dependent on a caregiver, humans are hard-wired to seek security and comfort.' (Allen 2011)

Where an individual suspects their 'real self' – who they are at their core – could threaten an attachment to others and thus the inherent security and comfort derived from this, they will endeavour to hide this aspect of themselves behind what they feel to be a more acceptable 'false self'. This can be both a conscious and an unconscious response.

Whilst this action may appear to be self-protective on the surface, helping them to fit in and become more acceptable, it is in fact a defensive action designed to help them avoid emotional pain and discomfort. Through this avoidance they do themselves the disservice of becoming something they are not whilst also avoiding the very experiences, albeit potentially uncomfortable, which will ultimately enable them to psychologically grow and develop.

'In other words, the false self does not set out to master reality but to avoid painful feelings, a goal it achieves at the cost of mastering reality.' (Masterson, 1988)

By encouraging the Personality and not seeking to control it, we get more investment from the individual. At HOME we still need the structure that a well-devised training programme supplies. However, our infrastructure has deeper roots based on Universal Values, which are then brought to life by the Unifying Principles.

'In previous companies I worked for there was an underlying, unspoken expectation that things would be done a specific way and there was very little room for manoeuvre or personal input. This led to myself and others feeling under valued and unheard, which created a very negative, unproductive culture. Despite having ideas about ways to develop the company, there wasn't the space or opportunity to express ideas. With HOME you are allowed to be yourself, in fact not just allowed but encouraged to be. We are always given the chance to express an opinion or idea in an open and honest environment.'

Jo, HOME Fundraising

Distortions at the level of the Personality Principle

Some individuals are great at working on their own, but in a group situation patterns of behaviour emerge that were not evident before. This is the result of what psychoanalysts refer to as 'intersubjectivity' (Stolorow, Atwood & Orange, 2002) – the idea that people are unduly and continually influenced by their relationships and environments.

Working alone, an individual's focus when performing a task is on applying what they bring to the job in hand (individual abilities and experiences, etc.) within the given environment. Whilst this is not completed in a vacuum, there are few interpersonal interactions to interrupt this flow.

An individual within a group, however, is biologically pre-programmed to shift their primary focus towards the social field. Concern for the task remains, but what now takes precedence are the verbal and non-verbal interactions and influences within the group which the individual cannot help but pay attention to, both consciously and unconsciously.

'How one person behaves affects how another behaves and his or her behaviour then influences the original person in a circular process.' (Gerhardt, 2004)

The consequences of this can be far-reaching within an organisation, both personally with individuals and professionally with the whole group.

We look to **create Conditions** rather than **control** actions.

When distortions occur at the level of the Personality Principle we focus on the external effect of everything we do, rather than the internal. For example, we're probably all familiar with a manager 'playing the popularity card' over the needs of the team. This then gets communicated to others; they intuit it in relation to performance: 'I am going to pretend to care and connect with you in order that you work hard for me and get the results.'

'Authenticity is there when the spirit is in line with the body and the words.' (Houston, 1984)

Any organisation, team or group is likely to be beset by distortions if the driving influence sits with the Personality Principle alone. We are not suggesting that we should discard our ego – in business a healthy ego is required. But the ego shouldn't be running the show. We should be giving more space to the part of us that empathises with others, not the part that focuses just on what we stand to gain personally. It's not something that always comes easily.

By trusting the Unifying Principles we have less need to protect our position or image, so we can respond more freely to others; then we find more Universal Values are in play. Without this mindfulness or trust, the decisions in groups will be made to fit in with the interest of the most senior person in the room and their insecurity, not necessarily what is best.

Now create a picture of an individual who focuses purely on the Personality Principle.

What would it be like to be them, to work with them, to be their friend?

Imagine the kind of company they'd create. What would it be like if they were running it? How would it treat people? What would it be like to work there and be managed by someone working purely from this Principle? What would the customer experience be like?

Now have a think about how you might focus too much on the Personality Principle. Where might it cause problems for you and those you work with?

Continue to do this exercise for the remaining three Unifying Principles. It will help you to really appreciate what each Principle brings and the consequences of continually emphasising one over the other.

Office Environment Audit

There are certain things which, if present on your desk or in your office/work space, will make you look, shall we say, as if you have a less than rounded personality. Try this exercise and see how you score at the end.

More than 2 staplers	5
More than two family photographs or any single family photograph over 11 by 14 inches (best saved for the grand piano)	10
Large selection of used biros in a faded receptacle	5
Cereal packet/s	10
Hip flask	15
Any motto on any plaque, however brilliant (save it for the shoulder tattoo)	15
A Smurf	10
Paper-clip chain	10
Your weight chart	20
Shelf of cacti	10
Protein shake powder tub	20
Fluffy computer monitor decoration (even if you're being ironic)	20
Abstract painting that doesn't have a flat surface	30
Object made of brass including the 'bankers lamp'	20
Novelty computer mouse	10
Snow dome paperweight	10
Newton's cradle	30
Plaque with your name and title, unless you are in Customer Services	40
Skateboard	30
Slide rule	20
Over-large expensive fountain pen (unless you are signing a treaty)	20
Baseball glove/boxing gloves	10
Bust of any great leader or philosopher (e.g. Napoleon)	30
Water feature	100
TOTAL	500

YOUR SCORE

Over 100: you may not be as well-rounded a personality as you think
Over 200: take your foot off the personality gas
Over 300: you may appear to others a little bonkers; the bust of Napoleon should be the first thing to go.

Let's be clear. We all have the potential to distort at the level of the Personality Principle, even with the best of intentions. Even wanting to overly please others or be popular with everyone can cause distortions. Think of the team leader who just wants to be liked by their staff. By failing to make their staff accountable to them they are likely to be manipulated and will create a situation to the detriment of the group. Don't get us wrong – we all like to be liked; but we all need to be aware of the inherent dangers and prejudices of letting this desire dominate.

David Brent (played by Ricky Gervais in the BBC TV comedy *The Office*) is the perfect example of a distorted Personality Principle, like an identity trapped in a carnival hall of mirrors. As viewers we can't help but attempt to identify with his actions, as we automatically do with any fictional character on screen, stage or page. Every time we reach out to him to empathise, we cringe as our Personality Principle steps back in pain – screaming 'Stop!' on his behalf. If we were acting and thinking like that, we would know, wouldn't we? We desperately hope we would and struggle not to identify, not to allow ourselves to accept this behaviour as a model. He reminds us always to keep half an eye on how we are coming across to others.

Some of Brent's distortions are that:
- he wants everyone to like him – a common distortion of the Personality Principle, and one we can all fall into from time to time if insecurity becomes our dominant emotion
- he believes he's viewed as a 'natural comedian', when in actual fact his jokes are usually way off the mark because he has no awareness of or empathy for others
- he wants to be everyone's mentor, even though he's clueless – again, his lack of self-awareness distorting him
- he feels that he's achieved the balance between manager and mate: being approachable but still having their respect – but nothing could be further from the truth.

There is a total lack of mindfulness, reflection and self-awareness. Like Brent we too can sometimes get trapped in the hall of mirrors, unable to see ourselves the way others see us. He's a tragi-comic figure, and a painful lesson to us all.

The Unifying Principles don't start the minute one sets foot in an organisation. They are the stuff of life and, as such, are developed over a lifetime.

Real growth, then, is knowing who we are, being grounded in that and not 'performing' for onlookers, not developing the personality from the outside, for the outside. The Unifying Principles seek to establish an internal harmony which then shows itself as an external harmony. All of the Unifying Principles look to achieve this balance. Without it, distortions will occur.

We're reminded of Salvador Dali's painting *Metamorphosis of Narcissus* (1937). Based in Greek mythology, Narcissus was a young man who loved only himself. The gods punished him for his vanity by letting him see his own reflection in a pool. He fell in love with the external image of himself without any reference to or understanding of his internal character, but died of frustration when he found that he could not touch it. Relenting, the gods immortalised him as the narcissus (daffodil) flower. Little comfort, we're sure.

One could interpret this painting as an individual who falls in love with their external persona and the image they present to the world. We believe that focusing on the internal is more lasting and far more rewarding.

It could be argued that this distortion is present in much celebrity culture today, not to mention personality-driven dictatorships – not that we are comparing the two!

Personality has its limits. It can only take us so far, particularly when we are managing large groups of people. The Personality cannot unify all the parts of us around it. As the need increases, either through greater responsibility or numbers of people, we can find unifying from this level impossible without distortions occurring. We may feel overwhelmed or stretched beyond ourselves. The need, then, is too great for the Principle we are responding from.

> 'I started off Personality managing. In other words I was putting too much focus upon the Personality Principle. It had some results but was unsustainable and in truth wore me down. Only when I went back to the Unifying Principles, internalised and understood those could I maintain a solid region that consistently performed.'
>
> Ben, Operations Director, HOME Fundraising

We noticed the breakdown of the Personality Principle as the numbers of staff grew within our organisation, particularly from 2006, when we more than doubled our regional offices. The manager working to the Personality Principle could no longer stay in contact with the whole group as numbers increased. The Personality was expanded beyond its natural 'field of influence'. A deeper Principle was needed to unify the group. Over time the lack of a deeper Unifying Principle will only split the group.

Personality and you

- In what ways and in what circumstances do you use your personality productively with your team or organisation?

- In what ways and in what circumstances can you be overly reliant on personality?

- In what way does behaving in this way serve you?

- What are the consequences for those around you?

- What might the long-term consequences be for your team or organisation?

- What can you do differently to address this behaviour?

Purpose Principle

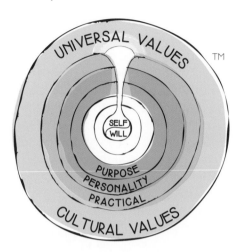

The Purpose Principle develops when we recognise the Root Need to understand our role in life and respond to it. When we experience the need for Purpose, we start to engage with and ask important questions about the narrative of our lives. There is a need to explore more deeply who and where we are, but most importantly who and where we want to be, where we feel our place in the world is, why we are doing what we are doing and the progress we are making; we recognise that we want to get the most out of our lives.

At the Purpose level we can 'fix the machine'. We know intuitively the process of our department inside out and its progress to our shared goal. We can spot distortions and rectify them. We can spot favouritism in ourselves and in others. We can see the difference between leading and controlling others and set the Conditions to adjust our behaviour and the behaviour of those around us. We try hard to operate with fairness and monitor our teams to do the same. We can recognise cliques and work to dissolve them.

We look for a good sense of the Purpose Principle from our more senior staff. They can be trusted at this deeper level to handle more complexity – whether intellectual, emotional or practical. This is not a matter of intelligence but maturity.

"Those who have a **'why' to live,**
Can bear with almost any **'how'."**
Viktor Frankl

The simple fact is that as leaders we don't have to be perfect, but if we choose to manage people we do need to get our stuff sorted; we've accepted the job, so with it we need to take the responsibility. Whether we know it or not, we are modelling versions of the Unifying Principles or their distortions all the time, so we need to be aware of them, and understand what they are and the impact they will have on us, our teams and our organisation as a whole. Not being aware will only lead to distortions in the group.

Just to be clear here: the Unifying Principles are not ways of acting. We are not asking people to perform with Personality or Purpose, striding around the office posing to one and all in a strange pantomime kind of way, in a caricature of the Unifying Principles.

Yes, if we want a chatty team, be chatty with them; that's a given – but if we want them to have real focus or commitment to a task, walking about the office 'demonstrating' won't help. If, on the other hand we genuinely and authentically bring our focus to the room, the team will feel that and the Purpose will manifest itself.

'What would you do if you were stuck in one place – and every day was exactly the same – and nothing that you did mattered?'

Phil Connors, Groundhog Day

Groundhog Day (Dir. Harold Ramis, 1993) is a beautiful, life affirming fantasy about grumpy, sardonic, self-centred weatherman Phil Connors (Bill Murray), who wakes up finding himself forced to relive the same bleak winter's day over and over until he learns how to truly live with purpose in his life. The reason Phil has failed to move on is that he's emotionally stuck and has been for a long while. He's in pain, but rather than examine his feelings, allowing reflection to lead him to a greater sense of purpose, he's taking it out on those around him.

Things begin to change for Phil when being emotionally stuck extends to him being temporally and physically stuck, too: a winter storm strands him and his weather team so they can't leave town. When his alarm clock goes off at 6am the following morning, mysteriously or magically, he finds himself living the same day again and again ... but gradually he begins to develop. He's being given a chance to see his thoughts, feelings, intentions and actions reflected in the Conditions he sets himself. He realises his impact on the people around him and slowly day by repeated day he changes: he moderates his behaviour, finds a sense of purpose, then refines and deepens it, discovering and acting to Universal Values.

Positive organisations and institutions within society look to reinforce these Unifying Principles and create good habits. In any organisation there are people eager to do more if given the opportunity. There is ample evidence – academic and anecdotal – that movements such as the Scouts and Guides improve self-esteem amongst the young, and most focused recreational activity gives people satisfaction through accomplishment. Indeed there is a blurring of the lines for some between recreation and a profession, such as musicians who may play recreationally or professionally. Motivated people also experience this blurring as their Purpose in life and at work are not conflicted. However, one outstanding example of the Purpose Principle in practice was the volunteer 'Games Makers' for the London 2012 Olympics, who learned a variety of new skills and helped create such an unforgettably magnificent atmosphere at the Games. Imagine being able to capture that passion of Purpose over the long term.

'I love my new job. Except it's not really a job. I'm doing this for nothing. And I'd do it again like a shot. My fortnight as a London 2012 games maker was the first volunteering I'd done and, to my amazement, I had a ball. I'm guessing it showed. After the fun had by all the Olympic volunteers and the fulsome plaudits from athletes, officials, spectators and the media, perhaps it's no wonder 100,000 new volunteers have signed up to help out in various ways nationwide since.'

Ann Mullard, *Daily Telegraph,* 20 August 2012

'For 10 of the 17 days of competition at London 2012 I have been an Olympic news service games maker ... We had a very tight bond. There's a sense of grieving in losing that. I feel intense pride in having been able to contribute to the Games. Like many others, I have not seen any live action, the work has been intense, often tiring and, in my case, the daily travel has been draining. But none of this matters compared to the great sense of achievement we can carry home each day.'

Tony Butcher, letter to *the Guardian,* 10 August 2012

When interviewing for new recruits for a management role within our own organisation, we ascertain how far the individual has developed and internalised the Unifying Principles. More than anything else, this gives us a clue as to the ability of the candidate to do well in the role.

Distortions at the level of the Purpose Principle

When the Purpose Principle goes wrong or distorts, we focus on controlling situations rather than responding to them; we look to rules and police them as hard as we can. Our focus moves from managing by Principles to managing by prescription. We can become dogmatic, overbearing and constantly frustrated with others. We can also, of course, have no sense of Purpose as we watch our teams run themselves and we lock ourselves away, managing from spreadsheets or by phone. Our connection with the Unifying Principles is temporarily lost.

We have had plenty of examples where we have had great leaders of small teams, people who were managing at the level of the Personality Principle but who have found it difficult to move beyond this, because none of us can manage larger teams on Personality alone. Senior managers need to recognise who is currently capable of managing at the level of the Personality Principle and who is ready to go beyond that. Not recognising this can have a huge negative impact throughout our organisations.

So senior managers should model the Unifying Principles that are missing in a team. This doesn't mean they will 'act' the Principles – i.e. walk about with Purpose, showing everyone what that looks like. Instead, they will work to their own Purpose. They may sit the manager down and realign them with their own Purpose in the job – and in life – asking them how they see their role fitting with where they want to be and what they want to be doing. This is not done in order to manipulate them, but with genuine interest and empathy. If the Purpose Principle is to be 'jump-started', it has to be genuinely brought to life in the manager. And senior managers who adopt this approach are working in a focused way to bring the Purpose Principle back.

Sure, there may be ways to get quick wins by replacing purpose with fear or short-term solutions to kick start action, but how long will that last? Engage the manager in their own Purpose and they can then engage again fully in the Purpose of their own role, the department and the company as a whole.

'I could see the region changing over a few weeks with the new manager that we had taken on. He used the control and command, carrot and stick. As much as I tried to shake him out of this, he would not have it, such was his belief in this way of operating. Before long he had created a region where favouritism and the distorted Personality Principle dominated. We couldn't keep the shifts up, as the turnover of staff was so great. There were still a few good performers, but overall the profitability of the region dropped through the floor.

'My job then was to model the Purpose Principle. This meant starting with fairness. I sat with the manager and our team leaders as we talked and reviewed them as a group and individually. Everyone was treated with the same level of courtesy and the same degree of honesty about my satisfaction with their performance. I was determined to model fairness and clarity.

'The manager picked up upon this very fast. It was so different from the way that he had been dealing with them. After a few visits the relationships with his staff had completely changed. They all knew where they stood. There was a growing appreciation for him. The shifts then grew and so did the amount of success we had per person. Purpose returned to the manager, the teams and the region.'

George, one of HOME's senior staff and most experienced managers

We need to be aware that the Purpose Principle is a common place for distortions related to power.

Smarmy salesmen are most obviously a distortion of the Personality Principle, but are also a distortion of the Purpose Principle. They will say anything to get what they want – their purpose is all about reaching a target and none of it about deeper values. We see all this smiling and laughter on the surface, but underneath we don't know who the person is at all. There's nothing real or authentic to them; they have almost disconnected from themselves, so focused are they on their goal. We might buy something from that person at a push but we won't feel great about doing so and we're certainly not going to take long-term advice from them. They may have no values; they will say anything, do anything, to sell anything.

'Working at HOME has taught me to ask myself why I do things in life, what I hope to get out of what I'm doing and where I'm going. This helps me make sure that I am doing the right things in the right way and for the right reasons, not just because that's the way things have always been done.'

Lisa, Head of IT, HOME Fundraising

But distortions need not always be obvious. They can occur at the Purpose level when we are unclear as to what our role as managers should be. Some managers think their role is purely to 'tell others what to do' and lose sight of actually 'doing'.

When a new recruit first joins HOME as a fundraiser, they are given clear instruction and steps on how to do their role at a Practical level.

The team leader will always be supporting them – modelling, encouraging them, giving them focus. So they do okay.

Now, let's say that person gets promoted to team leader. At first they stick by their good habits, but little by little over time these slip. They start to do less, to manage more. Rather than thinking that they can make more money, improve their figures and model well to the team, they think that they should focus on the managing rather than modelling; so now they only knock 30 doors rather than 150 per shift. What 'modelling' there was is dissipating over time to 'managing.' However, somehow they manage to get promoted to manager and the gap between managing and modelling gets even bigger.

As they progress up the ranks they consistently model to others that this is the idea. They move to the running of a regional office, by which point they have modelled this ideal of managing, not modelling, to everyone who works for them – in our case, to 100 people or so.

Eventually, the only people actually doing anything or holding the company together are those that are on the ground floor. Understandably, this results in tremendous resentment at one end of the company.

This is how some companies risk collapse.

Purpose and you

- Do you think you have identified your own personal Purpose in life? If so, what is it?

- If not, what do you think has prevented you from identifying it so far?

- If you are clear on your Purpose, how does the job you are in and the organisation you are working for complement those goals?

- Can you think of an individual or organisation you have ever worked with who had a distorted sense of Purpose? If so, what were the consequences for you?

- How clear do you think your own team is on how their Purpose fits with their work objectives?

- How might you support members of your team to get a clearer sense of their own Purpose?

Psychological Principle

The Psychological Principle recognises the Root Need to unify ourselves: to be whole and to feel complete. Self-awareness and mindfulness are key. We recognise when we are lacking something in ourselves and strive to understand and correct this. We are also aware of the impact of our mental states on those around us and see how important it is to own those mental states and hold ourselves accountable.

Without such accountability we risk allowing the side of ourselves that we do not own, in other words our shadow, to have a negative affect on us and those around us.

'The shadow (our darker side which contains unredeemed aspects) is integral to the human condition and needs to be integrated ...'

(Whitmore, 2000)

Subpersonality

Different subpersonalities, that we have developed throughout our lives to deal with or respond to various situations, are scattered across the psyche. We may have a strong inner-critic, or rebel, a warrior, artist, judge or saboteur: characters that help or hinder us depending on our awareness of them.

Our subpersonalities are formed in order to help us cope. However, they can lose their usefulness and instead hold us back or distort us.

The Unifying Principles provide us with a way to wrap our arms around our various and often incompatible subpersonalities, thereby anchoring them to our personal purpose and the wider narrative of our lives, giving them a role.

This is also the case in groups, where the various members – and their subpersonalities - will look to be unified by principle whether it is modelled or not by the leader. And of course, if it's not modelled by the leader it will be sought elsewhere or the subpersonalities will run amok. This then prevents the group from functioning .

The extent to which the leader has recognised, habitualised and internalised this principle will directly affect their ability to model it to others, and therefore unify and lead the team.

Subpersonalities are always in play in us and others. The Unifying Principles give us the rudder with which we steer ourselves and our teams.

Distortions at the level of the Psychological Principle

When the Psychological Principle distorts, we focus on the external, on how to control and manipulate others rather than focusing on ourselves. We are ignorant and not aware; mindless and not mindful.

Take, for example, a senior manager who unifies the team through her clear awareness of the Unifying Principles of Practical, Personality, Purpose and Psychological. She is successful and well-respected, with an excellent grasp of the practical nature of the roles within their team; she is a confident, collegiate personality modelling a strong Purpose to the group.

However, she is also currently experiencing some difficulties outside of the workplace and because she is human she naturally brings the effects of some of these difficulties into the workplace. Perhaps she is not able to communicate as effectively as usual. Maybe her concentration is not what it usually is.

This does not, however, mean that she is distorting at the level of the Psychological Principle – on the contrary, she is being human.

She has been open and honest with her team. She has explained that she is having difficulties that she recognises may at times impact on her presence within the workplace, but she will be mindful enough to know when and if her issue is impacting on her ability to make the right decisions for the team and act accordingly. This way she isn't pushing her problems out of the workplace, but neither is she bringing in her baggage. Remember we proactively ask our managers not to leave their humanity at the door. This is the Psychological Principle at work.

A distortion of the Psychological Principle would be far more likely to occur if the manager decided not to bring her humanity to work and to compartmentalise it away, allowing it to come out in bursts of anger at unsuspecting and undeserving team-mates or colleagues.

This situation leads to further distortions, as people form cliques to protect themselves from the unpredictable behaviour of the boss, and to speculate about the causes.

In the seminal children's picture book *Where the Wild Things Are* (Sendak, 1963), the infant protagonist Max attempts to deal with his anger and integrate the 'wild' side of his character in the safe confines of domestic imaginary play. He confronts and defeats the 'wild things' by becoming one and reigning over them. He has conquered his shadow and listened to his Root Need. Rather than being fearful of it, he has realised its creativity and potential.

Psychological and you

- How do you treat people – at work and at home? Is there any difference? If so, why?

- What mental and emotional baggage are you carrying which affects your behaviour and how you communicate and relate to others?

- What have you done recently that has had a positive effect on others?

- What have you done recently that has had an unnecessarily negative effect on others?

- What do you think the consequences of this were for others?

- How do you think that behaviour might affect how others perceive you?

- If you could have done something differently today, what would it be?

- How do you think being more mindful might change your behaviour and actions for the better in the future?

Philosophical Principle

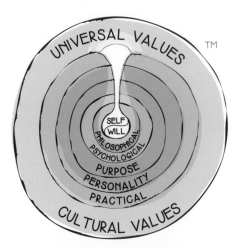

The Philosophical Principle recognises the Root Need for wisdom and meaning and responds to it. It is a call to unify ourselves around that wisdom. Examples of it abound in the great men and women that we are familiar with throughout the history of politics, philosophy, science, spirituality and the humanities. We are drawn to these figures and their stories, as they touch something very deep in us. Their inspiration still sets the Conditions for a better world often hundreds of years later.

Through these great figures we see leaders in tune with the Philosophical Principle who are able to create, communicate and sustain their vision. They have internalised each of the other Unifying Principles and are modelling a strong sense of Self and Purpose; they are objective observers but they also 'do'. This allows them to set and embody a clear Philosophy and align those around them with Universal Values.

When we work to the Philosophical Principle we see the big picture whilst also understanding the nuances and detail of that picture with absolute clarity. We seem less neurotic and more focused. We have a wisdom and insight which helps us reach the end goal in a way which is true to and connected with our Self.

Taking credit is less important than the enterprise being successful, the Unifying Principles being followed and our staff being fulfilled. We look to the health of the people and the organisation as our priority. We look to every level of the organisation and seek to connect the know-how and intelligence of the people and organisation with the Philosophy and Universal Values. The level of the Philosophical Principle is both intuitive and grounded.

Others buy in to our vision because it's a vision based on what's best for all. We realise that we don't own it; that real visions are shared and their success is dependent upon this.

Examples of the Philosophical Principle are scattered far and wide amongst characters in myth, fairy tales, modern novels and cinema – archetypes who serve as models for its embodiment.

When we were children we were first introduced to this figure as the wise wizard Merlin, the Fairy Godmother in *Cinderella,* or Mary Poppins. An unusual comparison we know – but we think it works, so bear with us. The Fairy Godmother, for example, is the custodian of what is right and wrong; she embodies the characteristics of the Philosophical Principle. She has her eye on the wider story and chain of events as she recognises that Universal Values are not in play as Cinderella is exploited by her sisters, seeking to rectify the distortion and so alter Cinderella's narrative. Within the Fairy Godmother's grasp is the power to restore balance and harmony and guide the key character. She has wisdom, insight and a plan. She knows that by acting in a certain way she will set up a chain of events that will lead to the happy ending. She is aware of all the tiny little movements she can make to change the course of events. She is working behind the scenes to pave the way for success. She knows the story, she is part of the story, but she has the ability to remain outside of the story as an objective observer. She is the conscience, the morality and the intent of the narrative.

'I have learned more about myself in the last seven years with HOME than I did in the whole 40 years of work before; more about how deep I can dig within myself, how profoundly I can think about what's really important as opposed to what just seems to be important.'

Robin, Training and Quality Officer, HOME Fundraising

But even working at the level of the Philosophical Principle, we still have to 'do'. Whether Nelson Mandela, Mahatma Gandhi, Dumbledore in *Harry Potter* or Glinda the Good Witch of the North in *The Wizard of Oz*, none of them sat there just talking a good job; they had to show as well as tell.

And so it is within our organisations.

When we bring all the Unifying Principles together, the Philosophical has a clear outlet in the Practical. The results of this will be far-reaching. Perhaps one of the most powerful notions of the 20th century was non-violent resistance as practised by Martin Luther King. He saw it not as passivity but as a real, powerful force.

King – who studied philosophy and theology and was a profound thinker – was inspired by the concept of Satyagraha (truth-force or love-force), which he saw could be applied to social reform.

He managed to practise this philosophy during the historic boycott of the buses in Montgomery that began with the arrest of Rosa Parks on 1st December 1955. In his own words, 'Hate begets hate, violence begets violence, toughness begets a greater toughness … we must meet the forces of hate with the power of love; we must meet physical force with soul force.'

The black community of Montgomery had to organise a taxi service to replace the bus so people could get to work, with volunteer drivers including church ministers. It was a huge logistical task. The Greek New Testament talks of a type of love called *agape* which, as King stated, 'springs from the need of the other person – his need for belonging to the best in the human family'. King saw *agape* as love in action.

It is a huge miscalculation to believe the Philosophical is detached from the Practical in business, and that thinking about something is detached from doing it.

Martin Luther King (2011)

Distortions at the level of the Philosophical Principle

Our work life is clearly *not* about endless meditation whiling away the hours lost in reflection. So one distortion of the Philosophical Principle is when we no longer 'do'. As vital as it is, sometimes a life built around reflection alone can lead us to lose touch with the Unifying Principles, to feel ungrounded and lacking in Will. The boundaries we rely upon can disappear and we lose touch with the Unifying Principles that keep us very much in the world and in the present moment.

Of course, we have to beware of the Messianic trap that's sprung when an executive – who already appreciates their high status by buying a wrist watch costing more than most of their workers' cars – now believes that their mature wisdom and self-knowledge puts them on the pinnacle of Maslow's pyramid.

They decide they are God's Appointed Board Director, so in touch with their being, so meditative and naturally beyond reading board papers. Accordingly they are now into the esoteric world of revelatory decision-making. No doubt they are living the dream, although every day is a fresh throw of the dice for the organisation. It is on a charismatic rollercoaster, as the executive, whose mind is now free of any financial detail, has only one obsession: who is loyal – not just to them, but to their vision shared with God or to the path or to whatever is deified over their muesli that morning.

You may think we're making this up, but rest assured in a lifetime in business you encounter these characters.

Distortions at the level of the Philosophical Principle will mean we create distortions at every other level.

The dangers of distortions at the level of the Philosophical Principle can be immense, as it talks to what is deepest in us: the Root Need for meaning.

In the world of fiction, think Voldemort in *Harry Potter* or the Emperor in *Star Wars*. And in the real world, of course, the likes of Pol Pot and Stalin.

We're sure we could all name a few from the world of business; our lawyers, however, have advised against it.

But we also find distortions at a Philosophical level where an organisation focuses on the needs of the shareholders alone and not on the people who work for it.

If we are caught up in building our own empire or the sole pursuit of profit, we may seem charismatic, efficient and successful and others may follow us. But our organisation will be a house of cards propped up by ego, ultimately doomed to collapse.

One of our favourite examples of how a distorted Psychological Principle can undermine everything beneath it is David Fincher's 1997 film *The Game*. Here we meet Nicolas Van Orton (Michael Douglas), a bloated millionaire control freak approaching his 48th birthday, experiencing deeply distressing flashbacks to his father's suicide. This state of painful reflection is a call from a deeper part of Van Orton to address the need for wholeness and substance in his life. He's middle-aged, rich, alone and dead inside; in many respects Nicolas is worse off than his father had been. So he's in crisis; he's blocked at the level of the Psychological Principle. And this, in turn, is distorting all the other Principles: his Purpose is hollow – he's practically a king anyhow, so what external empires are left for him to conquer? He's no longer engaging his Personality Principle – he has no meaningful relationships; and on the level of the Practical Principle all he really does is make more money. He needs a reason to snap him out of his malaise or he runs the risk of following in his father's desperate footsteps – right off the balcony of their mansion.

However, Nicolas is incapable of hearing and responding to his own Root Needs as his Purpose Principle is distorted, inadequate, starved and emaciated. So the need is restated by an external source – his younger brother, Conrad (Sean Penn). Conrad introduces him to Consumer Recreation Services, a company that offers wealthy customers the opportunity to play a life-changing game. After a period of reluctance, Nicolas accepts the call and soon finds himself tumbling down a metaphorical rabbit hole into a world where he loses control; he's threatened with the loss of his company, his fortune and, most importantly of all, his life.

The effect of these external threats is enough to engage Nicolas's Will. He starts to fight again, starts to live and to feel. He ignites his purpose, he has a mission, a solid foundation from which to rebuild his life and make sense of his whole world. And this in turn stimulates his Personality Principle as he's forced to break out of his self-created isolation. Finally, the film takes Van Orton literally over the edge, having him plummet back to earth into the bosom of humanity which he can experience from the vantage point of being invigorated with new life and purpose. At last, he has recognised and listened to his Root Needs.

Tiering

One Unifying Principle on its own won't bring results; they do not work in isolation. The real power of the five Unifying Principles for managers and leaders is in how they can influence and change the behaviour of teams and organisations as a complete model.

If we set up a lofty Philosophy in an organisation, but the way we behave undermines it, then the Philosophy becomes useless.

We could be charming and engaging; we could have good listening skills and be disciplined. But if we are all of those things and morally we are in a vacuum, behaving in ways that show us to be amoral human beings, we are just going to come across as hypocrites and disingenuous. After a while, one set of Unifying Principles undermines another one; an unsettling of one unsettles the rest.

Gerald Ratner, formerly chief executive of the major British jewellery company Ratners Group, made a speech in which he jokingly demeaned the company's products. A few simple sentences caused the company's near collapse and became known as the 'Ratner effect'.

At the Institute of Directors on 23 April 1991 he commented: 'We also do cut-glass sherry decanters complete with six glasses on a silver-plated tray that your butler can serve you drinks on all for £4.95. People say, "How can you sell this for such a low price?" I say "because it's total crap."'

Not only did his comments undermine products, but he made fun of his customer. After the speech, the value of the Ratner group plummeted by around £500 million, very nearly resulting in the firm's collapse. Here the Philosophy of the organisation was undermined – everything else went with it. But in addition to that, Gerald Ratner communicated a lack of values in relation to the business, and a lack of respect for his customers. He could no longer remain as the Philosophical Unifying Centre of the group; he no longer met the Root Needs of the organisation, so he resigned.

Unifying Principles as a route to natural leadership

First and foremost, we look to our leaders to be a solid, dependable centre; to be a person we can rely on to bring themselves wholly to the task – to reflect back at us the character traits, behaviours and attitudes that we intuit to be required to make us successful in our endeavours.

Our leaders can help us meet these Root Needs simply by having responded to them *in themselves*. A leader who has discovered and worked on *their* Purpose, for example, and has a strong grasp of why they do what they do in life, where they are going and how all the different parts of their life are connected and leading them in the direction they want to be going in, will have a natural 'broadcasting effect' on the people they lead. When the leader thinks, acts and feels with Purpose, their whole being exudes Purpose. By meeting that Root Need, they can't hide it. It is who they are – they can't help but be a model for the Purpose Principle. Teams, tribes, companies and groups have worked throughout history because their Root Needs have been met and modelled by the leader, providing them with cohesion, motivation and strategy.

In the dimension of 'individual growth' the Unifying Principles encourage deeper reflection and inspiration, releasing potential 'leadership'. Each Unifying Principle is a way of understanding leadership and a way of becoming a natural leader.

We take the view that true, authentic, natural leadership is not a form of imposition but an election by others. So we give our leaders respect because they've earned it, won our trust and have gravitas. They don't just take our respect as if it's owed, in the way that a soldier must salute his superior officer.

In our company, we have set the Conditions for open debate, allowing anyone to question behaviour irrespective of who it is. We are painfully aware of the times that one of our staff has called us to account.

We do not feel that it is **acceptable** to use **our position** to make our **point.** Our point should be **reasonable** and **compelling** irrespective of our position within the organisation.

Natural leadership (authenticity) is where we are genuinely inspired by an individual rather than following them through fear. Because, despite the controlling behaviour of many leaders, imposing our ego on others is not a long-term motivator. When we fall into this kind of behaviour we only model to others that leadership is about control and the infantile covering up of our lack of self-esteem. As leaders we are always modelling.

Leadership is an election by others.

The ability to manage at all five levels is a big ask and is actually rarely managed at all, but just an awareness of these five Root Needs in us and our organisations can change them for the better. If we had someone in senior management with no sense of themselves on a deeper level – someone who was caught up at the level of the Personality Principle, interested in being liked, focusing on their external image to those around them, reactive more than reflective – then fundamentally there would be no leadership whatsoever going on within the organisation. There would also be a huge risk that the most negative side of them would infiltrate into every area of the organisation and might show itself in over-dramatic behaviour or a serious scandal of one kind or another.

As leaders who are sensitive to the Root Needs of the group, we must take note of our feelings, being mindful and open as we listen, so we're more aware of what's being said in the 'subtext'. This is something that we will find far easier when we have internalised the Unifying Principles, as they give us an anchor – a place we can trust.

On the surface it may seem as though the need is for everyday things, so we set the Conditions to meet these, thinking that it will motivate people and solve the problems in our teams. We may set up competitions, games, work outings; we may even pay bigger bonuses. We might build in more breaks, try to be everybody's friend, but still we may fail to address behaviour that we find distasteful or counterproductive and in the process compromise our boundaries. By losing the connection with ourselves and our Root Needs, we lose our connection and clarity about the needs of the group. Unwittingly we then set the Conditions for the wrong needs to be met. We can start to get dragged around by the team. We may find that we are constantly looking to make them happy on a surface level rather than help them to be successful.

For example, a sports person might go to a coach to set the training Conditions to realise their Olympic dream. This will probably involve a tough regime: getting up early every morning, a healthy diet, time spent at the gym. The coach's job is to set the right Conditions for the realisation of the sports person's dream. The Conditions are set externally, then eventually internalised until they become part of the character of the athlete.

But if the coach panders to the athlete's own more trivial needs – like bad diet, less training, too much sleep – they won't achieve their goal. Eventually respect for the coach dissipates, as the athlete realises that their Root Needs are not being met, and the medal seems further and further away. The contract has been broken.

When this starts to happen in teams, we will find ourselves easily manipulated. Eventually the group will turn on the leader if they are no longer offering the external Unifying Centre or modelling the Unifying Principles. The group then can often become shadowy, undermining the group leader or trying to sabotage their efforts.

It may be that another member of the group becomes the Unifying Centre and is able to take the group forward, but this can be difficult for all involved if the title doesn't go with it. The group may recognise the real Unifying Centre but resentment will be rife from all angles. It is very difficult, then, to keep the team unified, positive and focused upon its agreed goal.

The **leader** must meet their **Root Needs** and **manifest** the Unifying Principles to **the group**.

There are jobs within any organisation where there is one Unifying Principle that is most dominant – but it doesn't mean that the others aren't there or needed. As leaders who have internalised all of the Unifying Principles we will intuitively know which the group requires at any one time. We will move comfortably between each of them, modelling what's best for the group to meet the needs of the moment – sometimes consciously, sometimes not. The Unifying Principle we work to may even change during the course of a meeting, guiding the group to focus on the necessary Principle, though this is not something we are controlling or manipulating.

Unifying Principles as a route to organisational change

The relationship between those in an organisation and the organisation itself would be well served if it was based upon the same Universal Values that all positive human relationships are based upon including trust, respect and genuine care for the well-being of others.

Sadly, some of us may find ourselves in organisations where this is not the case. Universal Values will be marginalised, staff turnover will be high, growth will be impossible, and unless the company can pacify people with very large financial benefits, then they will shut. People in these organisations will have one overriding Philosophy that binds them together: indifference.

But just being kind or working in a place where people care about each other clearly isn't enough. This can, if we are not careful, mean that we treat our work purely on a social level. The foundations here are clearly better, but still the end result can be the same. We are invested in the relationships but have no clear ways of contributing to or furthering our investment in the company. Ultimately, the organisation will not succeed.

By setting up organisations where the Unifying Principles are built into our language, personal motivation and training, we develop a continuing dialogue between our maturity, our intentions and actions and the organisation's outcomes. We develop a language and culture that everyone can relate to and a set of Principles that everyone can work with as they are based on our humanity rather than protocol and process.

By appealing to our humanity, the playing fields are levelled. Race, class, education or perceived power all become irrelevant as we hold ourselves and others accountable to the quality and clarity of our actions and interactions. We can look at all aspects of the organisation, including ourselves, and ask what Unifying Principles are missing. Modelling them then becomes the tool we use for change rather than paperwork, prescription or power.

We use the Values Universe model as a diagnostic tool, holding it up to the organisation and looking through it. In this way we are able to think about organisations without reference to the individuals involved. It's not about Sally in Finance, or Eric in Client Services, it's about where the Unifying Principles are within the organisation; where they are working and where they are distorting. So we can analyse an organisation as we would an individual:

- Where are the gaps?

- Where should the organisation be working from?

- What current problems and concerns are there within the business?

- What does this say about the Unifying Principle that is lacking or not as well developed as it might need to be?

- Do we lack Purpose or are we bickering, unable to own our stuff?

- Do we lack a clear vision or are we just not delivering at the level of the Practical Principle?

Signs of disintegration in the organisation, the group, even the individual or task, will make it clear that the next Unifying Principle needs to be developed and worked on. If we are aware of this within our organisations, we can change them or put them back where they need to be.

How is your organisation doing?

How do you think your department or organisation does in relation to the five Unifying Principles?

Take each Unifying Principle and its distortions and consider how much it is manifest in your department or organisation. Remember this is not a satisfaction rating but an honest assessment of how much each Principle currently plays a part. Rate it between 1 and 10, 10 being the highest. This will be a useful measurement to look back on in future months and give you an idea on how far your team has developed working to this particular Principle.

Now develop a list of five things you can do to make each Unifying Principle more manifest – these may be a combination of immediate action or longer-term projects.

Consider whether you have the right foundations and Conditions – a strong, shared Philosophy supported by Practical follow-up.

So what happens within a group or organisation when individuals start to model the Unifying Principles? It looks something like this:

1. Each member of the team habitualises, internalises and then models the Unifying Principles that they have recognised in their leader. It triggers their Will and connects them to a stronger sense of their Self.

2. This then triggers the Will of others in the organisation as they too begin to recognise, habitualise, internalise and model the Unifying Principles they have recognised in their colleagues. They, too, gain a stronger sense of Self in the process.

3. The Will of each and every person is galvanised into action as the Unifying Principles have a kind of viral effect on everyone who comes into contact with them.

4. The motivation of each individual and the motivation of the company are in harmony and hold each other in mutual respect. The organisation and each individual within it have a stronger and more authentic sense of Self.

5. Collectively each individual feels part of and invested in the whole organisation whilst remaining authentically themselves.

6. The organisation changes and flourishes through the growth and development of the individuals within it.

This whole process is not about being perfect, but about being perfectly us. This is clearly the ideal, but even by making an attempt changes to the organisation can be massive.

With this ideal process, the individual is engaged at every level. The organisation satisfies our Root Needs; it responds to our humanity. And when a team is motivated, and the members are connected to each other, there is harmony and direction; they are a force to be reckoned with. We're not saying as leaders we will always get it right – even within our own organisation – but through the Unifying Principles the Conditions will at least be set for us to be the best we can be.

Imagine the possibilities.

"To be **what we are**, and to become **what** we are capable of **becoming,** is the only **end of life."**

Robert Louis Stevenson,

Another story from Neil ...

I woke up one morning in my Brixton apartment.

7.30am and my routine had started: forty minutes of meditation followed by a good healthy breakfast and a short ten-minute walk to the boxing gym to get to training for around 11.

It was a strange job. I had found myself piecing together a living between sparring and training professional fighters during the day and playing guitar in the evening. I once played to three people. They clearly wanted me to shut up whilst they enjoyed their meal and conversation. I couldn't stop, though, as much as I wanted to; I was being paid. I tried to play quietly in the background so as not to disturb them, but it didn't work. After every song they clearly felt obliged to clap and make me feel better about the lack of audience by raining undeserving compliments down upon me, as they looked longingly at the door, hoping others would arrive to take over the cheerleading.

I wasn't looking forward to today.

It was normally a very friendly atmosphere at the gym. Most of the guys were good chaps. Even those that turned up looking mean soon found themselves in an atmosphere of mutual respect and friendliness. Professional boxing gyms can be a great leveller. Often there's a misunderstanding about boxers; that they are aggressive and like hurting people. This is not the case. You would find it very difficult to get a fighter to lift their hands to anyone outside of the ring. They are generally slow to anger and feel they have little to prove.

Andy and Martin were at the gym that morning. 'All set for today?' they asked me as I walked in.

'As I'll ever be,' I replied.

I was due to spar Big Paul. Big Paul learned to fight in prison. Big Paul was big. Very big.

Before sparring, Big Paul would always sit in silence in the corner of the room, his dreadlocks folded over his fingers as he looked at the floor. I never asked him what he went to prison for.

I stared at him, swallowing mouthfuls of fear (me, not him – I think he had very little fear of me). Paul looked slightly unhinged before sparring sessions. And after them, to be honest – one of the many reasons some of the other guys didn't like to spar with him. This wasn't helped by the fact that he treated every spar like a fight to the death. But it was my job. I had no choice who I sparred.

Sparring you see isn't about hurting people; it's about practising your skills. This fairly fundamental point seemed to have been missed by Big Paul. He hadn't lost a fight yet and was determined not to start now – not even in the gym.

The first two or three rounds, I was looking good. In truth, this meant I was standing up.

I was probably as fit as Big Paul. I sparred as much as he did, ran nearly as much, lifted weights. I knew my way around the ring and could survive pretty well. I hit hard, but I didn't have the height, reach or talent of Big Paul.

Boxing and the success of boxers can be seen in the context of the Unifying Principles. On the level of the Practical Principle, it's about keeping your hands up, your eyes on your opponent, one foot in front of the other, finding your range with the jab before throwing the other shots. Beyond this, your performance in the ring is massively affected by the deeper Principles. The Personality Principle, for instance, would determine how hard you had trained and how well you knew your own motivations.

The Purpose Principle would determine how well you put it all together and how much responsibility you took for your life and training as a boxer - the intention behind why you do what you do. In many ways the Purpose Principle deals with the Practical and Personality Principles, because when we take ownership of the whole process the rest often starts to slot into place. When this level has been effectively internalised, boxers talk about 'living the life' - in other words, sticking to the Principles in and out of the ring.

The thing with this is that the level of the Psychological Principle is never far away. Living every day being this mindful of the effects of your actions encourages the Psychological. You are forced to be mindful of habits that you have. You are forced to internalise the right Principles, question your motivation and build good habits until they become part of you. Lazy choices can lead to pain - nowhere is that more clear than inside the boxing ring where every move counts.

And when you're not aware enough on the Psychological level, your trainer acts as the Psychological: drilling the Principles into you until you begin to internalise them. Principles, Principles, Principles. You're persistently reminded of the Conditions that you are setting up for yourself and the vision that you are throwing away or undermining through the incorrect Principles that are being applied to your life in the ring.

They may not be as deeply internalised as they might be but as in all areas of life, the Principles are at play, conscious or not.

Paul punched me extremely hard in the middle of the face somewhere at the end of the fourth round.

Everything went white. Sounds got stretched and tinny; there was a rushing, whistling sound; voices sounded far off. I heard the desperate sound of a man breathing, a dying man (I thought) gasping for breath, louder and louder, more and more desperate, closer it came ...

The man was me.

Being knocked out isn't like in the movies. Everything disappears, you don't know where you are and you are desperately trying to hang on to any sense of yourself.

After a few seconds I came to and realised that I was still on my feet in the ring. This seemed like a terrible place to be, as another right hand found its way through my guard. It crossed my mind at this point to just leave, climb out of the ring and announce in a loud voice, 'I'll be going home now.' I could deal with the shame later, from a position of safety.

Staggering back, trying to focus on a world that had fragmented before me, I blinked again, expecting to find myself coming to on the canvas. But to my surprise, no, something was acting for me – my guard was up, my legs were strong. I was okay – in fact, not too bad.

I'd acted from the Principles when I needed them most. They were just there behind all the duress and fatigue, waiting for me to relax and allow them to do their work.

I would like to move this story into a kind of *Rocky* moment where the Principles helped me to climb back from the abyss, my true warrior nature taking over the fight as I remember some profound text I had read years beforehand that inspired my triumphant return on top.

Actually, the truth is I got battered.

And yet I finished the round and session, climbing out of the ring feeling strong. The Principles had done their job. I had a very clear experience of years of habits and internalising coming through and giving me something to trust in when I had nothing else to give.

This, I realised as I walked home at the end of the day, is what we mean by training: internalising the Principles so, even when you're not on top of your game, there's something there to guide you through and get you out the other side intact.

"Judge a man by his questions rather than his answers."

Voltaire

EMBARKING ON YOUR OWN VOYAGE

Okay, so we've covered an awful lot of territory over the last couple of hundred pages or so. But what's most important of all to remember is that the Values Universe model is already going on in all of us, our teams and organisations, to some degree or another. It's not something external, but comes from within.

Like the Scarecrow, Tin Man or Cowardly Lion in *The Wizard of Oz*, we may journey for miles in search of that one thing we've been looking for, only to find out we had it in us all along.

The key to working with our model is identifying the shape and form the Values Universe currently takes in your life. Get a sense of where it's working for you and where you could give it attention. Then apply the ideas to gently shift things into a better place .

What follows in this chapter is a list of specific questions to help you reflect on where you are now and the Conditions you have set for yourself and those around you. You'll be asked to consider where you have started to listen to and meet your Root Needs, to what extent you have unified around each Principle and where you could potentially do some more work.

Setting the right conditions

Every successful voyage begins with the examination and setting of Conditions. For individuals and organisations alike, this means placing Universal Values and a Philosophy that connects to these at the heart of everything we do.

The questions that follow will encourage you to reflect on the very foundations of the Conditions you are setting for yourself and for the people that surround you personally and professionally. They are the first stage in unifying our lives.

- What do you love about your life?

- What inspires you?

- What could do with some attention?

- What about your job?

- If you had a magic wand, what elements would you change and why?

- What would remain the same and why?

- In what ways would you consider yourself to be a tree in space – what 'nutrients' and 'atmosphere' do you lack to thrive?

- What elements of your life currently enrich you?

Your relationships

Now have a think about your current relationships – family, colleagues and friends.

- Jot down a list of your strongest relationships: the deepest, most meaningful, rewarding or positive.

- Look at all aspects of your life, past and present.

- What makes them work?

- What do you bring?

- Do they have anything in common?

Now do the same for relationships where you struggle to bond or communicate well.

- What is the impact of that on you and those around you?

- What would it take to move this relationship to the other list?

- What about the relationships within your organisation?

Playground cliques

We asked you these questions earlier in the book (p. 98) but in case you haven't had a chance to reflect upon them – they are big questions, after all – here they are again:

- Where do you see cliques in your organisation?

- What pay-off is there for the members?

- Are you part of one?

- What Conditions exist to support the continued existence of these cliques?

- What is it that connects or unites the individual members?

- What Root Need is not being met?

- What unrecognised or unresolved issues might have set the Conditions for these cliques to form and thrive?

- Consider ways in which you might re-set these Conditions and answer the Root Needs of the group more effectively.

Listening to your Root Needs

We all have five Root Needs at the level of the Practical, Personality, Purpose, Psychological and the Philosophical.

Remember: to set the right Conditions for you and your organisation to thrive, these Root Needs must be acknowledged. The next set of questions encourages you to reflect on them and be more aware of how well you are listening to and answering them. Without recognising these needs, you will be unable to unify yourself or the teams that you lead.

- How aware are you of each of these needs at the moment?

- How do they manifest?

- How are they calling to be met by you as an individual?

- How are you responding to that calling? Indeed, are you responding to it at all?

- What about in your teams and organisation?

- Are there needs that are currently being ignored?

- How often do you mistake these Root Needs and try to answer them with more money or promotion?

- Has this way of responding always helped the situation and, if so, for how long?

- What Conditions have you currently set to answer the Root Needs of the group?

- What Conditions might you set, or how might you adjust them in the future?

Think about all the touch points that people have with your organisation.

- Do you attempt to answer any Root Needs via these touch points? For example, in your branding, your recruitment, or induction programme, even in the contact you have with customers or clients?

- Be aware of this when you work through each of the Unifying Principles – how do you model the Principle and so respond to the Root Need?

Don't expect to be able to answer all of these questions at once; we hope that you'll spend time with them, maybe coming back to them over a number of weeks and months.

If you're not sure enough to answer any of the questions, if you're just guessing or wishfully thinking, then do some sifting and digging, look for any hidden assumptions and mull things over. As we've said before, just being aware of the Values Universe at work has an effect on us and the situation.

SIFTING AND DIGGING IN THE ASSUMPTION MINE

Assessing your current conditions

At work you might like to think about where else you need to look to assess the current Conditions of your organisation.

All things being interdependent, the real answer will almost certainly be everywhere … but some of the more obvious places include:

Board of directors and senior management

- Is your organisational Philosophy clearly defined and communicated, inclusive, with its roots in Universal Values?

- Is it important to people?

- Are they really living them or just parroting them?

As senior managers our role is to police and model the Philosophy keeping it alive and strong as part of the Conditions we are setting.

Recruitment process

- Does your recruitment campaign tap into the Root Needs of individuals?

This will potentially influence the kind of people that are attracted to your organisation and might make for a better match in the longer term.

- Are your interview questions and exercises designed to ascertain how far your new applicant has developed and internalised the Unifying Principles?

Think about what types of questions might help you, and make a note of them. More than anything else, this will give you a feel for the depth to which an individual can bring themselves to the role and do well in it.

Induction programme

- How welcome does a new recruit feel on their first morning?

- What steps are taken to make them feel immediately included and valued?

- Do the senior people within the organisation see this as part of their role?

- Are you greeting a new recruit with Universal or Cultural Values, or both?

- Who evaluates that, or do you make assumptions?

- Are Root Needs built into the fabric of the programme?

Managers

- What Unifying Principle do you see each working from, and are they modelling a deep enough Principle for their role?

- Do you have managers too caught up in the Personality Principle running big departments?

- Or are others working from the distorted Purpose Principle, with no strong connection to themselves or what they are doing there?

- Are your managers the Unifying Centre for their team?

- If not, who is, why and what effect does that have on the rest of the team?

- What Root Needs are being ignored?

Staff retention rates

- What do they say about the missing Unifying Principles in your organisation and the team or manager the member of staff worked with?

- Do you conduct exit interviews and, if so, how useful are they in terms of assessing the patterns and culture of your organisation?

- What Root Needs are not being met?

Staff complaint rates

- Are there any consistent comments or concerns which point to the missing Unifying Principle within your organisation?

- How does the manager or organisation respond to these comments, and is there a sense that they try to own their own shadow or are complaints brushed aside?

Financial targets

If the focus is purely on the end target without consideration for both how you get there and the impact of that on your staff, then distortions are bound to occur at some level of the organisation.

- Are you giving yourself and your business time to build strong foundations, or is your starting point profit?

- As a senior manager, are you solely looking after your own interests and unwittingly modelling this approach to a wider audience?

- Are you setting the Conditions for short-term gain at the expense of longer-term sustainability and profitability?

When looking at these questions, take your time. Whilst intuitive responses are valuable in reflecting our deeper gut instincts, care also needs to be taken to ensure these are neither 'knee-jerk' reactions nor a more superficial skimming of the surface. By taking the time to meditate on your answers, to be more mindful and to trigger the thoughts and opinions of those around you, a truer, deeper picture can emerge.

The further and wider you cast your net, the deeper your understanding and the more material your intuition has to work with.

Distortions

- Where can you see distortions most clearly in your life?

This is a hard question to answer because it takes a lot of honesty. Often we find when we ask this question that the initial response is 'nowhere', which is great. But sit with the question for a while, see what comes up and remember to apply Universal Values to yourself.

Be honest but compassionate. Show yourself some respect. The way you treat yourself when dealing with a problem is a model for the way you treat others. So treat yourself well.

- Have a think about all aspects of your life.

- Are there some areas that have fallen into certain patterns by becoming more or less distorted than the rest?

- What subpersonalities are in play?

- What's the pay-off for you?

And don't just think about yourself and your immediate influence.

What about your wider sphere: work, friends, groups, teams – even your whole organisation if you're a senior manager or director?

- Do people talk about each other behind their backs at work?

- Is there a culture of blame?

- If so, how do you respond to it?

- Do you collude, or do you pull people up on it?

- What subpersonalities do you see active in your workplace? Include your own.

Fortunately you don't have to be on your own with this – ask people and work with them to re-set the Conditions. If we ignore distortions, we will be unable to unify ourselves or our teams.

Creating a culture of Universal Values in your team or organisation

As we've already discussed, Universal Values have the potential to unify individuals and groups.

- What are the real values within your organisation? Not what's listed on your website or in your brochure, but all of them – both Universal and Cultural Values.

- Where are there distortions?

- What values are at the real heart of the organisation?

- Are they fixed and rigid, or are they a living, breathing entity?

- Do people understand them?

- Does the organisation live and work by them and do people know how to apply them to their role?

The danger here is being tempted to create a unique and different set of values to make us stand out from others in the marketplace.

Fight the urge to be different for the sake of it. Values are not a marketing exercise – they are part of who we want to be, what we hold most dear, what runs through the intention and Philosophy of our organisations, something we stand by in good times and in bad. It makes sense that your Universal Values may be similar to ours – don't be put off by that.

Show people that Universal Values are a part of how you do business every single day, and what they genuinely mean to your organisation and the individuals in it.

Give evidence of how you live by those values – easy to say, 'These are our values,' but much harder to demonstrate that you live by them in how you treat your suppliers, your staff, your customers ... even when the going gets tough.

Philosophy – the story of the values

Universal Values in isolation are unhelpful without also defining your own personal Philosophy. If you didn't do it earlier, think about it now.

- Write down three key statements at the heart of your personal Philosophy, including the Universal Values that are already important to you.

- What are the habits that you can adopt that will get you closer to embodying and internalising your Philosophy?

Now do the same for your organisation. Have a look at the organisational Philosophy you've written.

- Are the habits in the organisation moving it towards or away from the Philosophy?

- What does this do to everyone's belief in it?

Come back to this on a regular basis over the coming weeks and months to check how well your Philosophy has been embedded.

- If your organisation already has a Philosophy, is it alive and well?

If the focus is on the product or service, then remember it may need looking at again.

- How many people are aware of it and how shared is it?

Once the values and Philosophy of your organisation are in place, they act as a backdrop to your communications, meetings and daily tasks.

In terms of the Unifying Principles, your organisational values and Philosophy are a manifestation of the Philosophical Principle. If done well they can bring a new sense of vigour and will help to define its character and identity, giving each and every participant a unified sense of pride in the organisation.

The Unifying Principles

Recognising the Unifying Principles in our organisations enables us to bring the Philosophy to life – to go beyond empty mission statements that bear little resemblance to day-to-day experiences. So let us again try to recognise and understand the Unifying Principles and the needs they represent within us and all groups. The questions that follow will enable us to to see how unified we are as individuals and organisations around each principle.

Practical and you

Spend a few moments reflecting on the Practical Principle in your life.

- How do you meet your Root Need to *do*?

- How do you spend your time in and out of work?

- What practical skills do you have and are you working on new ones?

- What do you actually *do*?

- How much time do you spend on the practical day-to-day activities of your role? Is that enough time or too much?

- As a manager how much time do you spend on follow-up with your staff and teams?

- Do you know enough about what's going on in order to follow up effectively?

Personality and you

The Personality is the face we show to the world. If we want to unify our teams we need to know when to work from this Principle and when a deeper Principle is required.

- What's your face like? Is it loose and flexible, adaptable or ridged and fixed?

- What personality traits make you feel good about yourself?

- How well do you communicate what you think and feel?

- Are you a good listener?

- When listening, are you full of your reply or empty and able to hear what's being communicated?

- In what ways and in what circumstances do you use your personality productively with your team or organisation?

- How well do you communicate what you think and feel at work?

- How are these communications received by your staff, teams, colleagues or clients?

- In what ways and in what circumstances – both positive and negative – do you use your personality to affect a situation?

- In what way does behaving in this way serve you, and what are the consequences for others?

- What might the long-term consequences be for your team or organisation?

- What can you do differently to address this behaviour?

Purpose and you

Purpose is derived from what makes us happy, what inspires us, the narrative of our lives, what gives our lives direction and clarity about where we're heading.

- Do you think you have identified your own personal Purpose in life?

- If so, what is it?

- To what extent have you met it, and what could help you refine it or get closer to it? How does the job you are in and the organisation you are working for complement those goals?

- Do you bring your Purpose and intention to everyday tasks?

- If you haven't identified your Purpose, what do you think it might be?

- What drives you? This need not be a specific job or career path.

- Have you ever noticed someone who has brought a sense of purpose to the most mundane of tasks?

- What was the impact on you?

- Can you think of an individual or organisation you have ever worked with who had a distorted sense of Purpose?

- If so, what were the consequences for you?

- Think about the individuals in your team or people you work with on a daily basis.

- How much of their personal Purpose do you think they are aware of or have met?

- Does it seem to you that their Purpose is being met by the organisation?

- How can you ensure someone is more present in their role and help trigger their sense of Purpose?

Reflecting on these questions will support you and your team in unifying around the Purpose Principle.

Psychological and you

The Psychological helps us to own more of us, to be more reflective and so more aware of our humanity, and by extension what we bring to situations and relationships.

- What subpersonalities are active in your life (for example: the critic, saboteur, judge, carer, or people pleaser)?

- Which subpersonalities help and which hold you back?

- Do you respond to what's going on or try to control or manipulate it?

- What behaviour in others really annoys you?

- List the people and traits that affect you most.

- What is it about them that winds you up?

Now jot down any ways these annoying traits are present in your character. Be honest and compassionate. Most of us are surprised when we complete this exercise by the extent to which the things about others annoy and bother us, as we find many are traits we have buried and 'disowned' in ourselves – they are part of our shadow.

To be whole we need to accept these things in ourselves – not to be 'governed' by them or to ignore them, but to decide how we can be more aware of them and work to develop those areas.

- What mental and emotional baggage are you carrying which you know most obviously affects your behaviour and how you communicate and relate to others?

- What have you done recently that has had a positive effect on others?

- Or an unnecessary negative effect?

- How do you think that behaviour might affect how others perceive you?

Philosophical and you

Finally we arrive at the deepest of the Unifying Principles, the part that sits closest to our Self and Will, where we interact with the meaning and wisdom in our lives.

- What great leaders do you most admire?

- Who are your favourite writers, statesmen, thinkers?

- What is it about them that inspires you?

- What values and aspects of the Philosophical Principle do they model?

- What gives your life most meaning?

- Is it in the goals you have or your relationships?

- Do you have a philosophy, moral code, religious belief or spiritual practice that gives you a relationship with meaning?

- Do you live by Universal Values?

- How aware are you of the health and happiness of your team and organisation as a whole?

- How aware of and connected to the organisational Philosophy is each individual within it?

- Where do you think the Philosophical Principle is missing within your organisation?

- Why do you think that is?

- Who adds to the Philosophical Principle in your organisation?

- Do those that run your organisation embody this Principle or distort it?

- What can you personally do, and what responsibility do others need to take to strengthen the Philosophical Principle within your organisation?

PRACTICAL PRINCIPLE

doing,
practical output,
linking one task with another,
common sense,
tasks,
efficient

laziness,
not doing,
helplessness

PERSONALITY PRINCIPLE

personal uniqueness,
strong identity, interaction,
co-operation, listening,
understanding, communication,
empathy, honesty, internal

desire to please, cliques, falseness,
overly concerned with fitting in,
'top dog', manipulative, external,
playing the popularity card,
image

PURPOSE PRINCIPLE

fairness, focus,
understanding our role,
asking questions,
knowing who we want to be,
where we want to be,
our place in the world, why,
our progress and journey,
the goal and how we get there.

the goal in isolation, the wrong goal,
policing rules, dogmatic,
managing by prescription,
managing not modelling

● meeting
the need

● distortions

PSYCHOLOGICAL PRINCIPLE

whole, complete, aware,
own our mental states,
mindful, accountability,
own our shadow

not owning our own shadow,
anger, blame,
mindless, unaware,
subpersonalities

PHILOSOPHICAL PRINCIPLE

wisdom, inspiring,
sustained vision, creativity,
objective, observer, doer, clarity,
insight, intuitive, grounded, harmony,
balance, moral, humanity

not doing, endless reflection,
lack of boundaries,
short-term gain, dictatorship,
cowardice, conformity

Spot the missing Unifying Principle

Time to put your organisation under the microscope.

To start off, consider a team or department that isn't performing as well as you might like. They might not be as successful as they could, or it might be that they are disruptive or 'not playing ball' with other departments. It's not important why you think they aren't performing. This exercise will help you get under the bonnet and have a look at what's gone awry.

Mindfulness, **trust** and authenticity are the **remedies** for distortions.

Take each of the Unifying Principles in turn and, using the circles on the previous page as a starting point, write down all the ways in which you see aspects of them being modelled in the department.

Now do the same for distortions.

● What Conditions in the team or department distort the Unifying Principles?

● Are the Unifying Principles being modelled by the team members appropriate for their role?

● Who is the Unifying Centre of the team?

● Is this the person who you've employed to do the job?

● If not, what do you do about it?

Remember also to look internally to yourself as well as externally to others – is there anything you are modelling or not modelling which might be setting the Conditions for this?

Now that you've identified the missing Unifying Principle within the team or organisation, what can you do to model that and fill the Principle gap?

Think of ways you can bring the missing Unifying Principle(s) to your organisation. Just acting it out externally isn't going to do. It needs to be genuine and come from within, so be careful about setting out to consciously model it – it needs to be authentic.

Why's it going so well?

Now do the same for one of your best-performing departments or teams.

● What Unifying Principles are at play and where to enable it to function to its full potential?

To enable our organisations to fulfil their potential, we constantly need to remind ourselves to:

- Be mindful. Ask questions of ourselves and those around us.

- Check our motivation. Ensure Universal Values are at the heart of the questions we ask and the answers we give – if they're not, ask why.

- Be honest with ourselves and others.

- Trust our intuition. Trust that we can respond to our Root Needs authentically with the Unifying Principles and that the outcomes will be positive.

- Notice our responses.

- Be compassionate when we find fault, but don't let ourselves or others off the hook.

- Keep at it – this isn't a 'sticking plaster' to cover over a problem until it heals itself. This is more like a nutritious diet that will over time lead to a stronger, healthier organisation that has more life and vitality.

So, now that you've read most of the book, you'll want to get a sense of how well you have met the Root Needs we've talked about and how much you have internalised each of the Unifying Principles.

On an individual level, for example, we all have a Philosophy – whether it's conscious or not, developed or distorted – that informs our intentions. Our level of awareness of this Philosophy affects our relationships with others, how we look after ourselves and even how we work towards our dreams.

As a leader you'll want to know what effect you have on your teams, the principles you come from as a leader, and the principles that are manifest by the people around you.

You'll want to have an understanding of which principles your organisation is strong on and where they are weak; and what Principles are distorted and where they need some help. If your organisation has a clear Purpose Principle that's alive in the individuals and teams, the greater your ability to unify will be.

In order to help you bring all of this thinking together in one place, we've provided you with the following three diagrams. They are mirrors to help you reflect on where you think you are overall, as individuals and leaders, and for the organisations for which you may be custodian.

Use these tools whenever you want take off the blinkers and see clearly what's going on, looking first to the external factors in your life - at what you do - then moving to your more internal intentions - to who you are.

Refer back to some of the questions we have asked in this chapter to help you.

All you have to do is put a figure between 1 and 10 on the line between the area of concern and the centre (Unify), depending on how far you believe you have manifested the Unifying Principles in that particular area. 1 = very little (early stage Practical). 10 = completely (Buddha-like supreme manifestation). The areas we have included are only suggestions – you may wish to replace them with ones that are more relevant to you.

Once you have established where you are already strong and which Principles need developing, you're ready to set goals and implement them. Then step by step you can work towards meeting your Root Needs.

As each of the Principles gain a stronger foothold in the various areas of your life, you'll have the mirrors you need to help keep an eye on the progress that you, your teams and organisation make.

THE INDIVIDUAL

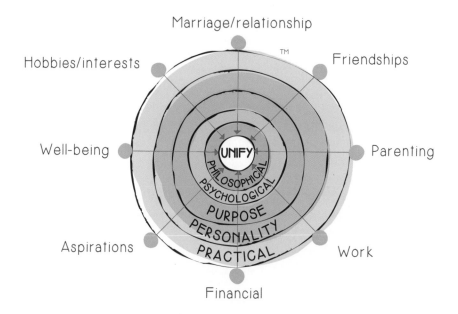

THE TEAM AND THE LEADER

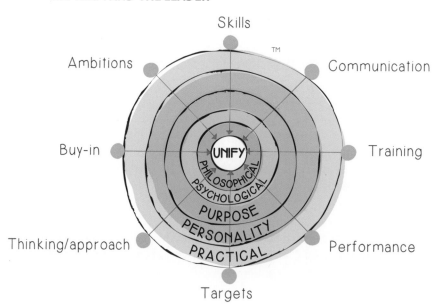

So, to conclude ...

We've taken you on a voyage to our Values Universe and hope it will encourage you to embark on your own.

As leaders it is part of our responsibility to listen to and answer the Root Needs of the group. This doesn't mean that the needs must be fully, perfectly, met every time; acknowledging their existence, working towards their resolution and beginning a dialogue with them can be enough to start you on your own and your organisational journey.

But don't let the context of the book restrict you. The Values Universe can be applied to every aspect of our lives, not just business.

Ultimately, being human isn't easy. But we can make it a lot harder when we try to meet all the expectations put upon us by ourselves and others to be more successful, fitter, better parents, better looking, less shy, more confident, thinner, bigger ... rather than listening more closely to our own Root Needs.

Our lives move so fast that we in turn want fast solutions to everything – from our relationships and finances to our psychological and spiritual well-being.

We habitually focus more on outcomes than on Conditions, not realising that the outcomes are in fact a result of the Conditions we set in every moment. In doing so, we unwittingly create the internal foundations to become anxious, agitated and ungrounded, so our relationships and work life can become inauthentic.

Before we know it, rather than setting the Conditions for us and others to shine, we become distorted. Unresolved issues that we carry around with us, as people, as leaders and as companies, seem to take on a life of their own as they block out our potential.

The Values Universe is not about conventional training, where people are stuck in a room for a couple of days and given a series of behaviours they are expected to follow.

This is about encouraging individuals to identify and tap into the Universal Values they will almost certainly share on some level with their colleagues; to support others to bring themselves more fully to their work; and in doing so help galvanise and develop our teams within a strong, human organisational philosophy.

Recognising that there are parts of us, our character, calling us to respond, be present and connect to our authentic selves can help us to experience ourselves and our lives more fully.

In our work the benefits of this are obvious. We can then take on the roles of leadership with maturity and drive as we learn to trust our authentic selves more fully, recognising that when we are more connected to our Root Needs we are then more connected to everything and everyone else. We are more unified – more alive.

We then model this to others, bringing to life the relationships and organisations we are involved in. In turn we encourage others to also live with more identity, purpose, wholeness and eventually meaning.

Instead of losing sight of our humanity we make it fundamental to all our relationships, our leadership and our decision-making as we help each other to become ourselves at our very best ...

"There is no passion to be found playing small, in settling for a life that is less than the one you are capable of living."

Nelson Mandela

HOMEWARD BOUND
– a brief history of our company

When we first started out with the business idea that was to become HOME Fundraising, we were pretty clear what we wanted to offer. Our core business – the door-to-door fundraising market – involves talking to people in their own homes about charitable causes and the option to support these through regular monthly donations. Traditionally it had been dominated by companies, both in the UK and globally, working to a business model based on commission payments for fundraisers (or sales agents, as they are often referred to). By running things this way you don't carry risk for an individual's poor performance; you can reward them with a commission if they do well, and you don't have to go through the hassle of directly employing them. After all, subcontracting is much easier.

Indeed, so attractive is this approach, it remains one of the most commonly adopted models for large-scale commercial doorstep selling across the globe (think utilities, broadband, etc.).

However, both we and our shareholders wanted to do things differently. We wanted to develop a business model that would give our clients the comfort of knowing that we were fully accountable for all of our staff – arguably an even greater currency in the fundraising world – whilst offering the opportunity to run large-scale campaigns signing up thousands of new donors and generating hundreds of millions of pounds for the causes we would represent. This type of model had not been achieved in Europe or, to our knowledge, anywhere else in the world, so presented an attractive gap in the market that chimed with our thinking. And, still to this day, HOME represents something unique within the fundraising market – an offering which has attracted and retained the support of many wonderful organisations, such as Oxfam, Macmillan Cancer Support, Save the Children, Cancer Research UK, British Heart Foundation and Marie Curie Cancer Care, as well as many others.

The story of HOME's construction begins in 2002 in London, where the foundations were laid in a dark, subterranean office with no natural light – note to aspiring entrepreneurs: light is a resource not to be underestimated! These first bricks were quickly followed by an office in Bristol (in an altogether more pleasing environment – we'd learned something by then); and subsequently Liverpool under a young Scouser (or Liverpudlian, for any non-UK readers out there) named Ian Dyson – now one of our leading lights in the senior management team.

Over the first three years we'd been busy, and by the end of 2005 we had built up three firmly established regions, each with an office employing a small management team and up to 50 fundraisers – all out knocking doors and raising over £10 million each year for causes as diverse as international development, child welfare, medical research and protection of the environment.

In these early days the business was separated in quite specific ways. Neil was travelling around developing the regional fundraising teams and Dom was out visiting clients, explaining our new approach and drumming up business. So whilst Neil was in Liverpool, Dom would be in Oxford; and when Dom went to Manchester, Neil would be in London. Unsurprisingly, perhaps, for any new business spreading itself across half the country, we barely saw each other.

Added to this was the considerable pace at which everything was growing and evolving around us. Every week, day, hour even, there would be new considerations to think about; further conversations with regional managers about what was and wasn't working; and a constant refinement of how we were doing things and how we were communicating our philosophy to our growing internal and external audiences.

Finally, as anyone involved in start-ups will testify, we were doing all this with a backdrop of huge financial considerations and pressures, too. Shareholders had significantly invested in the company and held their nerve through the many ups and downs in the early days, and for this we owe them much respect and gratitude. Their ongoing support was extremely important, as our innovative new business model meant that, whilst on the plus side we carried greater responsibility and accountability for our employees, the downside to this was that we now carried the risk for all of the people we employed. If large numbers of staff underperformed, we weren't simply able to offset this against not paying them commission. Poor performance at any level meant we would lose money, and fast. The simple equation of not meeting targets, coupled with paying out more in wages and other expenditure than we were able to generate in fees for the donors we were recruiting, meant the pressure on cash flow could become overwhelming, to say the least. Similarly our reputation was being forged on delivering a quality product for which we attached a premium, so the last thing we could do, or indeed wanted to do, was drive targets with no regard for the potential negative effects on the service we were delivering.

All of these factors meant we had to learn quickly, react even quicker and apply every ounce of business savvy we had honed through the many long days (and nights – belated apologies for which to Rachel and Nina, our long-suffering partners!).

Familiar questions included: What should we charge clients, and what guarantees should we offer? How should we remunerate and incentivise our staff? How should we develop our training to reflect our growth? Included within this right from day one was our shared idea that alongside the practical need to make the balance sheet stack up was the belief that it was not only a tangible product and service we were selling but the values and principles that sat behind these. Although we didn't know it back then, these would be the factors that would ultimately lead us to significant growth and the sustainable success of the company.

And if you're tempted to write us off on the grounds that we work in a sector where from the outside 'doing good' is assumed to be a motivator in itself, think again. Like any industry we are surrounded by good companies and bad, best practice and poor. Besides, if you ask anyone who has ever been involved in fundraising how easy it is to find donors, you're likely to be met with an awkward smile and a shake of the head. Knocking on doors in all weathers, you're not always met with a welcoming smile. Motivation can be hard for the 2,000 staff we employ. It's a tough industry to work in. But still our model works.

Three years in we needed to make the decision to either 'stick' or 'twist' and grow further. We knew that, in order for our organisation to grow and be successful in the long term, we would have to set the right conditions throughout the company for this to happen. We would need to encourage the right people to either come into the organisation from the outside or take the decision to promote relatively young people from within on the understanding that they would be able to step up to the greater levels of responsibility asked of them. And we needed to continue to develop our understanding of what was at the heart of a team's successes – and failures.

Our Values Universe model – the lead character in this book – was under construction and our focus with managers became increasingly more about managing to principle, or the 'why' behind what they were doing, and not simply the practical processes associated with their role.

Throughout our management infrastructure, we aligned managing to principle with developing and encouraging a greater understanding of how the behaviour of managers and leaders affected the performance of the groups or departments they led.

As this deeper level of understanding took hold throughout our operations, we had the confidence to 'twist' and play the hand we'd worked hard for. We expanded our services into new regions – Manchester, Sheffield, Nottingham and Birmingham in 2006 – whilst proudly maintaining the quality and consistency of our service and meeting the growing demand from clients.

Interestingly, the received wisdom in our industry is that expansion equals a decline in quality, so we were more than happy to have bucked the trend – not least because that would have been our key USP out the window in the blink of an eye!

For us, however, the development of the thinking behind the Values Universe and its application within our company is key to our continued improvement in all Key Performance Indicators (individual sign-up rates, cancellation rates, gift levels, complaints ratios, to name but a few).

As financial turmoil rocked societies across the world in 2007 and 2008, we continued to expand significantly with four new regions: Newcastle, Southampton, Exeter and Leeds. Now, we're not saying we've got all the answers to the global financial crisis. However, we do think it's important to note that when external conditions get tough a business needs more than its targets and financial incentives to fall back on. In our case the economic climate influenced a general decline in the level of voluntary donations to charity in the UK, so the challenges were as tough as they'd ever been.

Given the economic climate, it also made sound financial sense to spread our costs across a wider base. From 2009 through to today we have opened offices in Glasgow (2010), the central support service in Worthing (2010), Norwich and Aberdeen (in 2011) and Coventry (in 2012). As we write this midway through 2013, we are looking forward to a summer in which an unprecedented 2,000 committed fundraisers will be out on shift talking to hundreds of thousands of potential donors and generating immeasurable levels of support for the fantastic causes we are fortunate to represent.

We have also recently taken our operations to India and we look forward to the next decade being one with a global flavour!

So, from its humble beginnings in that subterranean office back in 2002, HOME has built itself into an international operation that has raised £400 million of charitable donations to date. We have scaled up by over 100% in some years, without compromising our brand, reputation or profits – and in a troubled financial climate where talk of triple-dip recessions is not uncommon, we have grown and grown. The model we have developed along the way works personally, professionally and financially, delivering sustainable results. But it needs to be modelled continuously.

Acknowledgements from Neil

My partner, Rachel, has been amazing. The number of weekends, evenings and straight 20 hour writing sessions I've done in the last year or so would have tested anyone's patience. I would very much like to acknowledge her contributions around style, feel and content; as always she has amazing taste and intuition. Thank you to my mum who helped me when I got stuck with the text. She was so proud that I had managed to write a book that, at the hospice, she had the nurses gather around whilst showing them proof copies. At a time when she was very ill, she was still able to remember whole pages of text in her head and re-order them. Remarkable. Thanks to my sister, who had more authenticity and values than any human I have met. I miss you both terribly. And to my dad for being his usual supportive, good bloke self. I love you all.

REFERENCES

Allen, J.R. (2011) Relational practices and interventions: neuroscience underpinnings. In Fowlie, H. & Sills, C. (eds) *Relational Transactional Analysis: Principles in Practice.* London: Karnac Books

Assagioli, R. (2000) *Psychosynthesis: A Collection of Basic Writings.* Massachusetts: The Synthesis Center

Berne, E. (2009) *Transactional Analysis in Psychotherapy.* London: Snowball Publishing

Butcher, T. (2012) I feel intense pride as a gamesmaker. *The Guardian.* 10 August. http://www.theguardian.com/society/2012/aug/10/intense-pride-gamesmaker [last accessed 17/02/2014]

Campbell, J. (1949) *The Hero with a Thousand Faces: The Collected Works of Joseph Campbell.* New York: Pantheon Books

Churchill, W. We Shall Fight on the Beaches. House of Commons, London, UK. 4 June 1940

Deming, W.E. (1982) *Quality, Productivity and Competitive Position.* Massachusetts: MIT Press

The Game (1997) Film. Dir. Fincher, D. USA: Polygram Filmed Entertainment

Gerhardt, S. (2004) *Why Love Matters: How Affection Shapes a Baby's Brain.* London: Routledge

Groundhog Day (1993) Film. Dir. Harold Ramis. USA: Columbia Pictures

Hillman, James (1997) *The Soul's Code: In Search of Character and Calling*. New York: Bantam Books

Houston, G. (1984) *The Red Book of Groups and How to Lead Them Better*. London: The Rochester Foundation

Hudson-Allez, G. (2009) *Infant Losses; Adult Searches: A Neural and Developmental Perspective on Psychopathology and Sexual Offending*. London: Karnac Books Ltd

Innocent Drinks http://www.innocentdrinks.co.uk/us/careers [last accessed Nov 2012]

Judge, L.W. (2010) Developing a Mental Game Plan: Mental Periodization for Achieving a 'Flow' State for the Track and Field Throws Athlete. *The Sport Journal*. Vol 13, No. 4. http://www.thesportjournal.org/. [last accessed Dec 2013]

Kabat-Zinn, J. (1994) *Wherever You Go, There You Are: Mindfulness Meditation for Everyday Life*. London: Piatkus

Luther King Jr, M. Christmas Sermon on Peace. Ebenezer Baptist Church, Atlanta, GA. 24 December 1967

Luther King, M. (2011) *Stride Towards Freedom: The Montgomery Story*. London: Souvenir Press

Man vs Wild (2007) Television. Dir. Shearman, S. et al. UK: Channel 4

Marlatt, G.A., & Kristeller, J.L. (1999) Mindfulness and meditation. In W. R. Miller (Ed.) *Integrating Spirituality into Treatment: Resources for Practitioners*. p 67-84. Washington: American Psychological Association

Maslow, Abraham H.; Frager, Robert D.; Fadiman, James, *Motivation and Personality*, 3rd Edition, ©1987. Reprinted by permission of Pearson Education, Inc, Upper Saddle River, NJ.

Masterson, J. (1988) *The Search for the Real Self: Unmasking the Personality Disorders of Our Age*. New York: The Free Press

Mullard, A. (2012) London 2012: Olympic volunteering was a pleasure and a privilege. *The Daily Telegraph*. 20 August. http://www.telegraph.co.uk/lifestyle/9487624/London-2012-Olympic-volunteering-was-a-pleasure-and-a-privilege.html [last accessed 17/02/2014]

NHS National Health Service UK http://www.nhs.uk/Conditions/
Depression/Pages/Symptoms.aspx [last accessed Feb 2014] &
http://www.nhs.uk/conditions/antisocial-personality-disorder/Pages/
Introduction.aspx [last accessed Feb 2014)

The Office (2001) Television. Dir. Gervais, R. & Merchant, S. UK: BBC

Plato (2007) *Republic.* 3rd edn. London: Penguin Classics (originally
written 380BCE)

Sendak, M. (1963) *Where the Wild Things Are.* New York: Harper & Row

Steare, R. (2009) *Ethicability: How to Decide What's Right and Find the
Courage to Do It* 3rd edn. Roger Steare Consulting Ltd

Stewart, I. and Joines, V. (2012) *TA Today: A New Introduction to
Transactional Analysis* (2nd edn). Melton Mowbray and Chapel Hill:
Lifespace Publishing

Stolorow, R.D., Atwood, G.E., & Orange, D.M. (2002) *Worlds of Experience:
Interweaving Philosophical and Clinical Dimensions in Psychoanalysis.*
New York: Basic Books.

The Texas Chainsaw Massacre (1974) Film. Dir. Hooper, T. USA: Vortex

Whitmore, D. (2000) *Psychosynthesis Counselling in Action.* 2nd edn.
London: Sage

INDEX